media in
art

media in art

classroom materials for moving media in art at key stage 3

introducing practical work for GCSE media studies

Tony Carroll

BRITISH FILM INSTITUTE

bfi

BFI PUBLISHING

Acknowledgments

Tony Carroll and the BFI would like to thank
all the teachers who piloted and developed
the materials, in particular Peter Coleman,
Eileen Flynn, Kathy Stonier, and the
participating schools:
George Orwell School, London; Holy Cross
Intermediate and Ifield Community College,
Crawley; Claverham Community College,
Battle.

We would also like to thank Bradley Gray, a
Fulbright Scholar, who reviewed the pack,
interviewed the classroom teachers and
provided us with valuable comments, during
his placement on the BFI's 1995 MA
programme.

Credits

We acknowledge the use of pictures and stills
from the National Gallery, BBC, BFI Stills,
Channel 4 and ITV and films, television and
videos courtesy of the Arts Council, BBC,
Channel 4, London Electric Arts, MTV,
Transit Films, Vector Television, and
Warner Bros.

Sources for printed material are acknowledged
throughout.

Media in Art was assisted by a grant from the
Nuffield Foundation.

Photocopies of pages can be made freely for
educational purposes.

Cover illustration: *The Supper at Emmaus*,
Caravaggio, 1601, reproduced by kind
permission of the Trustees of the National
Gallery, London.

contents

Module C	**A Question of Identity**	

introduction

New media and new forms of expression are emerging that provide exciting possibilities for pupils in the art room. *Media in Art* focuses on the need to find some ground between art studio practice, conceptual understanding and the growth of interest in media education among young people. *Media in Art* aims to provide a critical approach for classroom practice in art lessons and a practical approach for media studies course work.

The media play an important part in our everyday lives. Television, radio and newspapers communicate what is happening outside our front door; we use video and photography to record events; films and music are important to us as forms of expression and entertainment.

In *Media in Art* we are advocating and presenting exciting possibilities for the linking of media education and art, in ways that will develop pupils' practical and critical visual art work. The National Curriculum allows for a range of media to be used in art, such as photography, film and video. Use and critical application of these media enrich the curriculum and increase the tools available to the visual artist, working alongside and within fine art, three-dimensional studies and textiles.

We hope that teachers and their pupils will feel inspired to extend classroom practices through traditional media forms of drawing and painting into audio-visual media, language of film, video and multi-media technologies. Through the activities in this pack, we aim to unlock the creative potential of our pupils, in a way that is relevant to them culturally and technologically.

Using the pack

Activities in the pack are designed to allow the exploration of a variety of traditional and modern media technologies. Drawing and painting play central roles in the process of visual research. The intention is to offer photography and video activities, and to introduce digital image work. Our other main aim is to provide pupils with opportunities to produce meanings from different kinds of visual image, including paintings, photographs, prints, comic strips and film stills.

We have structured the activities but hope to have left room for teachers to be selective in their use of them. Each module is based on the integration of analysis and practical work in keeping with the National Curriculum Order for Art. It is assumed that departments will have their own assessment procedures based on the National

Curriculum for Art, but we have included a National Curriculum reference for each activity, and an Assessment Table at the end of each module, to guide departmental administration.

About the modules

The pack is divided into three modules, one for each year of Key Stage 3 – Years 7, 8, and 9. They are designed to encourage progression through the Key Stage. The units will substantially fulfil GCSE Media Studies practical coursework requirements.

Module A
Throwing Light on the Subject

explores dramatic lighting in *film noir* photography and baroque painting through an investigation of *chiaroscuro*. Pupils are asked to light the subject from different points of view and subsequently organise images of their own into a sequence from a given starting point, using photography and/or film (video).

Module B
The Art of Film Design

involves the study of posters, film stills and clips from German expressionism as well as modern experimental work. This leads to design work in response to briefs based around a contemporary animation, *The Sandman*, which was itself inspired by German expressionism.

Module C
A Question of Identity

shows how television channel identities are created, very often using and borrowing from a range of popular and unpopular cultural references. Through analysing and making logos and idents for their own channel identity, pupils gain deeper insights into a more complete process of planning, researching and making within a specific context and for an audience other than themselves.

Learning objectives

We believe that students' learning in art will be greatly enhanced by the study of key aspects of media education. By working through the activities in this pack, pupils will be able to:
▶ understand the pictorial conventions and meanings of art by making and analysing images
▶ use a variety of media materials, tools and technologies to draw with, and begin to experiment with processes and techniques
▶ understand the conventions of pictorial realism and, where possible, explore alternatives
▶ make connections between different kinds of art through visual and written research
▶ begin to show greater awareness of the social uses and meanings of art in different contexts.

Tony Carroll and Julian Bowker 1996

video
contents

The video clips are designed for use with the support materials in the teachers' guide.

Module A
Throwing Light on The Subject
Video clip 1: *Digital Still Life*, 1989
Malcolm Le Grice
8 min 19 sec
Part 2, Activity 2.3

Video clip 2: *Abstract Cinema*, 1993
Interview with Malcolm Le Grice,
Arts Council
1 min 30 sec
Part 2, Activity 2.3

Module B
The Art of Film Design
Video clip 3: *The Sandman*, 1991
Paul Batty, Colin Berry,
Ian Mackinnon, Vector Television
10 min
Part 1, Activity 1.1

Video clip 4: Camera Angles in
The Sandman
2 min 20 sec
Part 1, Activity 1.1

Video clip 5: Colours and shadows
in *The Sandman*
2 min 44 sec
Part 1 Activity 1.1

Video clip 6: *The Sandman*:
The producers talk about its making
Paul Berry, Ian Mackinnon
3 min 34 sec
Part 2, Activity 2.2

Video clip 7: Excerpt from *The Cabinet of Dr Caligari*, 1919
Robert Wiene, Transit Films
3 min
Part 2, Activity 2.2

Video clip 8: Extract from the
opening to *Metropolis*, 1926
Fritz Lang, Transit Films
1 min
Part 2, Activity 2.3

Video clip 9: From the opening to
Blade Runner, 1982
Ridley Scott, Warner Bros
1 min
Part 2, Activity 2.3

Video clip 10: *The City*, 1991, 16mm
(Arts Council 'One minute film series' first shown on BBC2's *Late Show*)
1 min
Carole Bellon, Bella Kerr
London Electronic Arts
Part 2, Activity 2.3

Video Gallery (Module B)
Part 3, Activity 3.3
Stills of children of Holy Cross
School, Ifield, Crawley at work on
poster design and set construction
1 min 4 sec

Module C
A Question of Identity
Video clip 11: BBC2 idents 1992
3 min 52 sec
Part 1, Activity 1.1

Video clip 12: MTV logos 1994
2 min 15 sec
Part 1, Activity 1.2
M Art History, Colossal Pictures,
Kirk Henderson (US), 10 sec
MTV Frank 'M' Stein, Sean Burns
(US), 24 sec
MTV Street, Bill Jarcho (US), 10 sec
Gitano, Cathryn Marshall (UK),
10 sec
MTV Bosch, Voltaire (US), 15 sec
Adam and Eve, Isabella Bannerman
(US), 10 sec

Potato Head, Varga Studios
(Hungary), 10 sec
MTV Magritte, Richard
Reiss/Bannerman (US), 15 sec
Far Out Man, Ged Haney (UK),
10 sec
120 Minutes, Neil Bousfield (UK),
21 sec

Video clip 13: *Gargantuan*, 1993
(Arts Council 'One minute film series'), 16mm
1 min
John Smith, London Electronic Arts
Part 2, Activity 2.4

Video clip 14: *Sundial*, 1993, 16mm
1 min
William Raban, London Electronic
Arts
Part 2, Activity 2.4

Video clip 15: *Eerie*, 1993, 16mm
1 min
Sandra Lahire, London Electronic
Arts
Part 2, Activity 2.4

Video Gallery (Module C)
1 min 5 sec
Part 2, Activity 2.4

Video Gallery (Module C) 3.1
3 min 14 sec
Part 3, Activity 3.1

Video Gallery (Module C) 3.2
15 sec
Part 3, Activity 3.1

Video Gallery (Module C) 3.3
24 sec
Part 3, Activity 3.1

Video Gallery (Module C) 3.4
20 sec
Part 3, Activity 3.1

National Curriculum References

8b select and record observations and ideas, and research and organise a range of visual evidence and information, using a sketchbook

8c experiment with and select from visual and other source material to stimulate and develop ideas for independent work

8d select from and experiment with materials, images and ideas, and extend their experience of a range of materials, tools and techniques

8e select from and interpret visual elements and realise their intentions in a range of media

8f modify and refine their work, and plan and make further developments in the light of their own and others' evaluations.

9a recognise the diverse methods and approaches used by artists, craftspeople and designers

9b identify how visual elements are used to convey ideas, feelings and meanings in images and artefacts

9c relate art, craft and design to its social, historical and cultural context, e.g. identify codes and conventions used in different times and cultures

9d identify how and why styles and traditions change over time and from place to place, recognising the contribution of artists, craftspeople and designers

9e express ideas and opinions, and justify preferences using knowledge and an art, craft and design vocabulary

throwing light on the subject

The aim of this module is to offer pupils the chance to explore different media, using lighting to make their own images. (Torches, anglepoise lamps or candles are cheap and effective substitutes if studio lighting is unavailable.)

Pupils will develop their drawing, photography and film skills by responding to a range of visual resources which are provided. They will also learn to use simple lighting and framing techniques, and to analyse how these conventions communicate meanings, by considering the effects of lighting on body postures, dress and sets.

The activities allow pupils to interpret art produced in its own context and also to go on to make connections between painting and film.

Summary

The module, which should take a maximum of twelve weeks to complete (two hours per week, allowing time for evaluation work), is divided into two parts:

Part 1 Drawing on Light

Pupils draw a lit still life, photograph figures, collect secondary source information and 'read' a variety of images which have been selected for their intriguing use of lighting.

Activity 1.1:
Drawing Light and Shade
120 minutes

Activity 1.2:
Lighting a Dramatic Pose
120 minutes

Activity 1.3:
Reading Stills
120 minutes

Part 2 Art into Film

Pupils apply their knowledge of simple lighting techniques to create a 'What Happens Next?' sequence.

Activity 2.1:
In the Frame
120 minutes

Activity 2.2:
Narrative Image Sequences
240 minutes

Activity 2.3:
Non-narrative Image Sequences
240 minutes

drawing
on light

Objectives *In Part 1, pupils will*

▶ draw a still life from direct observation

▶ construct images using simple lighting methods, an SLR stills camera and a tripod

▶ understand and apply the term *chiaroscuro* to their own work

▶ make connections between the painterly convention and the lighting techniques used in photography and film

Activity 1.1
drawing light and shade

National Curriculum reference
8a develop ideas from direct experience and imagination, and select, record and analyse from firsthand observation

Resources provided
Activity Sheet 1.1:
Lighting in Context
Information Sheet 1.1:
Lighting Techniques and Types
Image Bank 1.1:
Lighting a Dramatic Pose

Resources required
Darkened room; anglepoise lamps, or candles; paper and pencils/charcoal

Method
Set up a still life drawing activity for the whole group. Dark pencils and/or charcoal should be used. If possible, darken the room and use simple lamps or candles to light the still life from below and to the side.

Introduce the session by referring to Activity Sheet 1.1: Lighting in Context. With the group, discuss the statements on the sheet and the effects created by the lighting in the two images.

This observation exercise not only gives pupils useful practice in recording and analysing but also facilitates efficient classroom management. While the majority of pupils are still drawing, one small group at a time can set up a photo 'shoot' as described in Image Bank 1.1: Lighting a Dramatic Pose.

Follow up
Pupils can build up their own bank of 'found' images from magazines for use in subsequent work. They should look for figures and 'still lives' which have been observed from above or below. If possible, they should try to find examples which demonstrate the use of various lighting angles.

This may be an appropriate time to introduce Information Sheet 1.1: Lighting Techniques and Types, which describes the techniques most commonly used in film and television and will also give pupils the language to use when talking about them.

Activity 1.2
lighting a dramatic pose

National Curriculum reference

9e express opinions and ideas and justify preferences using knowledge and an art, craft and design vocabulary

Resources provided

Image Bank 1.1:
Lighting a Dramatic Pose
Information Sheet 1.2:
Key Words

Resources required

As for Activity 1.1, plus an SLR stills camera and a tripod

Method

Before starting this activity, discuss Image Bank 1.1: Lighting a Dramatic Pose, with the whole group. Ask pupils where the light source has been placed in each image. Also, how does the background suggest a particular location or situation?

Ask pupils to work in small groups to prepare a simple photo 'shoot'. (Rotate the groups and return pupils to the still life drawing activity in Activity 1.1 when they have taken their pictures.) The objective here is to photograph a class member using light sources from various directions. If the subject is able to pose in a simple but dramatic way in an interesting location (for example, in front of a bookcase or near a stairwell), the creator may be able to suggest a storyline within the still image.

Discuss Information Sheet 1.2: Key Words with the group and help pupils understand how they can apply the term *chiaroscuro* to their photographs, drawings and paintings.

Follow up

This activity may be taken a stage further. Pupils can combine the still life work produced earlier with images of figures (either 'found' from magazines or photographed) to create a final composition, perhaps depicting a scene around a table. A photocopier will help pupils reduce or enlarge the various elements of the collage as required.

Technical advice

When lighting a subject using an anglepoise lamp, torch or candle in a darkened room, it is important that the SLR camera should remain still, to gain maximum clarity. It is possible to obtain a relatively cheap tripod, but a camera can be supported on another object, for example a step ladder. It is best to use 35 mm colour print film as it can be developed quickly, and relatively cheaply. There should be no need to use a flashlight. Of course, black and white pictures may be more atmospheric, but it can be difficult, and also expensive, to have such photographs developed, unless a school darkroom is readily available.

Activity 1.3
reading stills

National Curriculum references

9b identify how visual elements are used to convey ideas, feelings and meanings in images and artefacts

9d relate art, craft and design to its social, historical and cultural context, e.g. identify codes and conventions used in different times and cultures

Resources provided
Information Sheet 1.3:
Shot Sizes and Framing
Activity Sheet 1.2A, B and C:
Historical References

Method
With the group, study Information Sheet 1.3: Shot Sizes and Framing and discuss the language used to describe the different camera shots.

Then, using the notes below and the questions provided, guide pupils through an analysis of the still images provided on Activity Sheet 1.2A, B and C: Historical References Sheet.

Activity Sheets 1.2A, 1.2B and 1.2C Historical References Sheets:

A – The Graphic Novel
The graphic novel is a visual story book using comic strip pictures and text. Many artists use high quality drawing and design skills to produce shot angles and perspectives which often look like those found in some films. Many of the characters as well as the illustrators have cult followings.

Pupils should discuss in groups how the action shown in this page from *Violent Cases* is restricted to one small dramatic moment, focusing on the exchange of money. The reader sees the whole scene from the boy's upward-looking point of view. What effect does this create? Encourage pupils to discuss the different ways in which they might read the story sequence. Some might read it from top to bottom or from left to right. Others might scan or select different clusters of images and interpret their possible connections.

B – Chiaroscuro Painting
Caravaggio, a seventeenth-century Italian painter, became well known for his dramatic use of lighting in dark paintings of biblical subjects. He discovered that he could manage to paint light and shade to give the effect of cast shadows. This technique brings objects and figures alive by making them appear three-dimensional. Examine, for example, the shadows cast by the plates of food in *The Supper at Emmaus*.

Caravaggio exploited the dramatic and emotional potential of chiaroscuro. Later, this convention became popular with photographers and film makers. One modern photographic director, John Alton, studied paintings of this period to gain inspiration for his *film noir* lighting techniques and effects (see, for example, a film called *The Big Combo*, 1955).

C – Film Noir
The film *The Blue Gardenia* (Fritz Lang, 1953) is a good example of a style or genre known as *film noir*. This term is used to describe a number of mystery or thriller films produced in the years after the Second World War in America.

They all share the same strong visual style, using artificial lights to produce dark shadows and dramatically lit faces and bodies. The main technique used to achieve this effect is known as *key lighting* (see Information Sheet 1.1: Lighting Techniques and Types). The mood created in these films was 'dark', reflecting a sense that the lead characters were likely to come to a bad end.

The look of *film noir* owes a great deal to the influence of immigrant directors, particularly from Germany, such as Fritz Lang, who was working in Hollywood during the 1940s. These directors brought with them methods and ideas common among European artists and film makers of the 1920s and 1930s. It is possible to detect, for example, conventions and techniques from the expressionist movement in many mainstream post-war films. (See Module B for an analysis of specific elements of expressionism, such as distortion of line and colour.)

art
into film

Objectives *In Part 2, pupils will*

▶ investigate the concept of *mise-en-scène*

▶ devise and film/photograph their own visual narrative sequence

▶ learn about storyboards and film/photograph a scene from a storyboard

---

Activity 2.1

in the frame

National Curriculum reference

8d select from and experiment with materials, images and ideas, and extend their knowledge and experience of a range of materials, tools and techniques

Resources provided

Information Sheet 1.3: Shot Sizes and Framing
Image Bank 2.4: Illustrated Storyboard

Resources required

Video or stills camera; an empty space into which pupils can move in order to be photographed or filmed; light sources (for example, lamps, candles, spotlight)

Method

The main objective is for pupils to discover what happens in a fixed camera shoot, that is when figures and objects are moved within a frame.

As a whole group, study Image Bank 2.4: Illustrated Storyboard and Information Sheet 1.3: Shot Sizes and Framing. Identify the different camera positions used and what the point of view is in each shot. Discuss where and how often the camera angle changes. Where are the light sources and how are they used? Now discuss how pupils will have to act out, light and film the sequence illustrated on the storyboard in order to make it more sinister and mysterious.

Pupils should then video or photograph the sequence shown in the storyboard. Or, they could try one or two of these suggestions:

▶ A figure walks into a dark or empty space. The light is switched on and the figure suddenly looks up.
▶ A figure is sitting in a chair. The neon street lights outside the window flash on and off.
▶ A torch/candle follows a hand which is holding an object.

It might be useful to find a space (such as a stairwell or a drama studio stage) into which light can be directed from above, in order to create the effect of harsh top lighting.

Pupils should be encouraged to experiment by asking the actors to move in and out of the frame and therefore in and out of the darkness.

MODULE **a** TEACHER'S NOTES

Activity 2.2

narrative image sequences

National Curriculum references

8e select from and interpret visual elements and realise their intentions in a range of media

9d identify how and why styles and traditions change over time and from place to place, recognising the contributions of artists, craftspeople and designers

Resources provided

Activity Sheet 1.2A:
Historical References –
The Graphic Novel
Information Sheet 1.2:
Key Words
Image Bank 2:1:
Film Noir – The Blue Gardenia
Image Bank 2.2:
Chiaroscuro Painting –
The Supper at Emmaus
Image Bank 2.3:
Blank Storyboard
Image Bank 2.4:
Illustrated Storyboard

Resources required

Light sources (as before); SLR stills camera and tripod; darkened room; video recorder; video camera; computer (if available)

Method

The objective is for pupils to devise a 'What Happens Next?' sequence from a given starting point (see Image Bank 2.1: *Film Noir*, or Image Bank 2.2: Chiaroscuro Painting), or to continue developing Image Bank 2.4: Illustrated Storyboard. Pupils should work in small groups to draw (graphic novel), photograph or film (video) the next few shots in the story. They should aim to use between six and twelve frames, or up to 30 seconds of video, and they can

★ If pupils decide to develop the storyboard on Image Bank 2.4, they could draw the next few shots in the story, revealing a bit more (but not all) of the sinister 'thing'. They should produce 6–12 frames and include notes about sound effects and music. There must be a variety of cu/ms and long shots.

create any one of the following:

▶ a photo story extract
▶ a page from a graphic novel
▶ a storyboard for a film or video*
▶ a computer-aided video sequence

If pupils are creating storyboards for film or video, you may wish to insist on carefully drawn versions; if, however, they are creating a photo story, a page from a graphic novel or a computer-aided video sequence, they may provide a number of drafts, all of which can be kept as evidence of process work in sketchbooks.

Narrative sequences

Before the photographers and director begin work on a film, they plan out each scene using a storyboard. This is a sequence or series of images and instructions that shows what will appear in front of the camera in each scene of the film, that is the *mise-en-scène* (see Information Sheet 1.2: Key Words). Recap Activity 2.1: In the Frame as the practical realisation of *mise-en-scène*.

Before the class starts work on the photo story extract, graphic novel or film or video, it may be worth spending some time exploring the function and purpose of storyboards. As an introduction to the idea, ask pupils to draw the process of opening a present as quickly as they can, in six sketches. Pupils should not worry about the quality of their drawing skills for this activity: the aim is to encourage them to vary the shot sizes, to think sequentially, to decide what to include in each frame and how to hint at the whole by drawing part of something.

Before pupils start work on their photo story, graphic novel images or storyboard sequence, discuss with them again the page from the graphic novel on Activity Sheet 1.2 – A and Image Bank 2.4: Illustrated Storyboard, using them as examples of storyboards. How will *they* organise their sequence?

a How will they create atmosphere (through lighting, light and shadows, or through abstract manipulation of the image)?

b How will they create a sense of motion (through rapid shot changes, the camera's movements, or the subject's)?

c Will there be different shot sizes and framing (through a close-up or tilted angle or wide angle)?

d Will there be more than one scene in the sequence, for example, a different scene in the same space occurring simultaneously (cutting back and forth from one scene to another)?

Pupils may like to experiment with dressing up and researching appropriate locations and props for their sequence to *The Supper at Emmaus* or *The Blue Gardenia*. Discuss what gestures and facial expressions they will need if they are to create a sequence in keeping with the painting or still. A subject's look, for example, depends on what caused the subject to look in that direction and on what the subject is looking at.

Pupils need to be aware that in a narrative sequence the moment presented in one shot must cause the next shot to occur in a logical and coherent manner. This flow of events gives the impression of reality or truth. It might help to reinforce this point by encouraging pupils to complete a blank storyboard (Image Bank 2.3) to break down the scene into shots for their narrative sequence. They can refer to Image Bank 2.4: Illustrated Storyboard for guidance.

Discuss the technical aspects of using lighting and the way it can serve to suggest a meaning. Lighting the scene should be consistent and carefully constructed. Use an anglepoise light or torches if no drama or video lights are available.

Technical advice

Pupils' sequencing work could be recorded using an ion camera, which allows images to be stored on a computer disc and then called up immediately on a monitor. This facility will help when attempting the next activity. (See the Technical Guide on p.70 for further information on photo stories and video work.)

Activity 2.3

non-narrative image sequences

National Curriculum references

See Exceptional Performance criteria in the National Curriculum Document for Key Stage 3 (p.10)

Resources provided

Video Clip 1 :
Digital Still Life,
Malcolm Le Grice, 1989
Video Clip 2:
Abstract Cinema
Activity Sheet 2.1:
Digital Still Life

Method

First watch Video Clip 1: *Digital Still Life* and discuss the questions about the images and music given on Activity Sheet 2.1. Explain that non-narrative means that a sequence does not have to follow a logical, causal or linear path. By studying this video clip, pupils should become aware of the way in which artistic conventions or rules can be broken. (Le Grice rejected the narrative structure as a way of making images of the world.)

Now watch Video Clip 2: *Abstract Cinema*. Discuss how Malcolm Le Grice defines his type of 'abstract' art. Pupils will see how it is possible to experiment or 'play' with visual form.

Pupils can now attempt to create a non-narrative sequence, using either the still life they created for Activity 1.1 or a scene specially set up for this purpose. This will be easier to achieve if they can store their images on a computer using an ion camera. If the computer is equipped with an animation programme, they may be able to incorporate shots of the still life prepared in Activity 1.1 to produce a sequence.

If pupils' images have not been stored on a computer, they can achieve rhythmic and repetitive shots by stop-starting the record button on the video camera. They could also try fragmenting the perspective and point of view by moving the camera to various positions or by showing only parts of the observed scene in close-up.

Pupils can combine music with these images in one of two ways: they can either edit the images to a particular soundtrack, or they can create music to accompany the images, once they have edited them.

This activity is designed to extend pupils' work by inviting them to use the scenes and images they have just created to produce a sequence which breaks narrative conventions. Pupils are already aware of narrative and non-narrative conventions as a result of watching music videos and films, from reading books and graphic novels, and from playing video games. The techniques and effects of Abstract Cinema are now being 'raided' by young animators and other film makers, particularly those working in the 'indie' and 'dance' music video field. This exercise should help them to build on and consolidate that knowledge.

assessment
table

Learning outcomes	Activities	Evidence	Assessment methods
Make images using drawing and photography skills	Part 1: Activities 1.1, 1.2 Part 2: 2.1, 2.2, 2.3	Sketchbook: still life drawing; photo of figure; image sequences	Evaluation of a product
Understand terms such as *chiaroscuro*, conventions and narrative	Part 1: Using Information Sheet 1.2 – Key Words	Written notes – Image Bank 1.3; practical work	Question and discussion; evaluation of oral work
Produce a visual narrative sequence using stills or moving images	Part 2: Activity 2.2	Photographs; video	Evaluation of a product
Employ media technologies such as still camera, tripod, simple lighting and/or computer to produce stills in sequence	Part 1: Activities 1.1, 1.2 Part 2: 2.1, 2.2, 2.3	Pupil self-assessment, recording what technologies they used	Observation
Begin to appreciate that there are alternative ways of sequencing images	Part 2: Activity 2.3	Video and/or computer work	Observation; evaluation of a product
Work effectively on their own	Part 1: Activities 1.1 Part 2: 2.3	Still life drawing; non-narrative sequence	Observation
Contribute to group work	Part 1: Activities 1.2 Part 2: 2.1, 2.2	Photo shoot of figure; in-the-frame shoot; narrative sequence	Observation; evaluation of oral work
Evaluate their learning, making explicit their knowledge of chiaroscuro lighting and narrative conventions	Keeping records, notes, organising a sketchbook, and applying knowledge to practical activities	Pupil self-assessment	Question and discussion; evaluation of product(s)

lighting
techniques
and types

Photographers, film makers and television producers use various lighting set-ups and techniques to create different effects.

Backlighting
This involves using a hard spotlight behind the subject at 30 to 60 degrees to light the head and shoulders. If used without other lights, a backlight will cause silhouettes.

Underlighting
This means lighting the subject from below in order to distort the features. Underlighting is often used in horror films.

Toplighting
A light placed directly above the subject will emphasise features such as cheekbones. Toplighting is often used in comedy films.

To create the standard lighting set-up, a photographer or film maker needs three lights (or lamps):

the key this is the main light source that will illuminate the whole scene; it should be placed above and to one side of the subject at 15 to 45 degrees. A hard key light will produce sharp shadows on the other side of the subject.

the backlight this is a hard spotlight placed behind the subject at 30 to 60 degrees, lighting the head and shoulders.

the fill this is a soft flood light placed below the subject on the other side and closer to the camera, to soften the shadow or even 'fill' it completely.

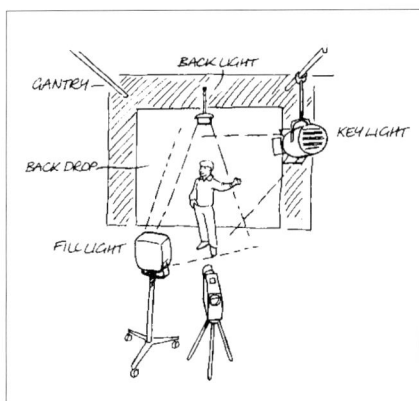

Above:
Standard lighting set-up (from *Hands-on!*, Roy Stafford, BFI, 1994)

Right:
A single directional light: low key lighting (pupil at George Orwell School, photographed by members of the group)

Far right:
Key, backlight and fill lighting: a classic studio portrait (pupils at George Orwell School, photographed by members of the group)

lighting a dramatic
pose

Look carefully at these photographs. They were taken by small groups of pupils at Ifield Community College, Crawley. The pupils were interested in suggesting a possible storyline in their images by carefully framing their shot, and by choosing the most suitable and effective lighting direction, dramatic pose and background setting. They based their ideas on the imaginary film stills series by the American photographer Cindy Sherman. You can find examples of her work in *Cindy Sherman* (The Whitechapel Gallery, 1991).

Above, top centre
and right:
Joanne Harrison.
Far right top:
Dhvani Patel.
Far right below:
Michelle Icombe.

lighting
in context

Begin by discussing the following statements:

▶ Light falling on a subject can make it appear mysterious, beautiful or even ugly. It can reveal texture, detail and it can emphasise form.

▶ Light can conceal, mask and obscure vision for particular reasons, and can influence how audiences respond to an image.

▶ Light can create compositional relationships for the camera.

▶ Light can develop atmosphere or mood.

▶ Light can establish environmental associations suggesting location – a forest, church or prison, for example; it can isolate a subject with a spotlight.

▶ Light can provide visual movement – a torchlight in the dark, flickering sunlight in a moving train interior.

Adapted from *The Techniques of Lighting for Television and Film* by Gerald Millerson (Focal Press, 1993)

Now study these two images and answer the questions below.

Top:
Example of a lit still life (photograph by T Carroll)

Bottom:
Film still from *Devil in a Blue Dress* directed by Carl Franklin, 1995

1 Which statements from the list above can you apply to these images?

2 What kind of effect does the lighting create in these two images?

key words

Conventions, *chiaroscuro, mise-en-scène*, narrative and non-narrative: these are all terms that you may come across when reading or talking about paintings, photographs, graphic novels and films. But what do they mean?

Conventions

A *convention* is a rule, or accepted way of doing something or behaving. For example, in England it is a convention to shake hands with someone when you meet them for the first time.

Low key lighting

In films and photography, there are conventions about lighting. When we see a typical lighting effect, such as the sharp contrast of *low key lighting*, we associate it with films that are mysterious or full of suspense. This is the accepted or conventional way of lighting such films.

Chiaroscuro

Chiaroscuro is a term that can be used to describe the deliberate combination of light and shade within an image. (It comes from the Italian, chiaro = clear, oscuro = dark.) Chiaroscuro was first used to describe lighting effects created by painters; it is now also used with films.

Mise-en-scène

In film, the use of lighting to alter or enhance visual appearance is one element of what is known as *mise-en-scène*. It has been defined as:

'All the elements placed in front of the camera to be photographed: the settings and props, lighting, costumes and make-up and figure behaviour.'
(From *Film Art* by David Bordwell and Kristin Thompson, McGraw-Hill, 1979)

Although *mise-en-scène* is a term which has been developed in relation to the cinema, there is no reason why we cannot apply it to other visual images, such as photographs, drawings and paintings.

Narrative

In a *narrative* sequence, the moment presented in one scene must cause the next scene to occur in a logical and coherent manner. This gives an impression of reality or truth.

Non-narrative

Non-narrative means that a sequence does not have to follow a logical, causal or linear path.

shot sizes
and framing

The basic shot-sizing and framing terms used in film and photography are illustrated right:

Illustrated by Miguel Sapochnik, 1996

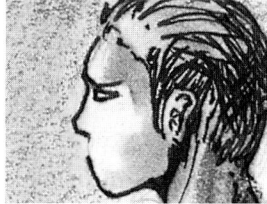
Big close-up
B.C.U.

Over the shoulder shot

Close-up
C.U.

Moving subject – framed with space to walk into

Medium close-up
M.C.U.

High angle (looking down)

Medium shot
M.S.

Low angle (looking up)

Medium long shot
M.L.S.

Tilted frame

Long shot
L.S.

Very long shot
V.L.S.

the graphic novel

Look at the page below and consider the following questions:

1 What kind of mood or atmosphere is created by the shadows in these images?

2 How many changes in shot size, framing, angle and point of view can you find (for example, close-up, medium shot, long shot)? Describe the whole sequence using this language.

3 What effect do the illustrators create by focusing on the moment when the hands exchange the money? Why did they use a series of shots? And why use close-up shots?

4 What effect do the illustrators create by framing the man in close-up in the last shot? Why is he shown looking downwards?

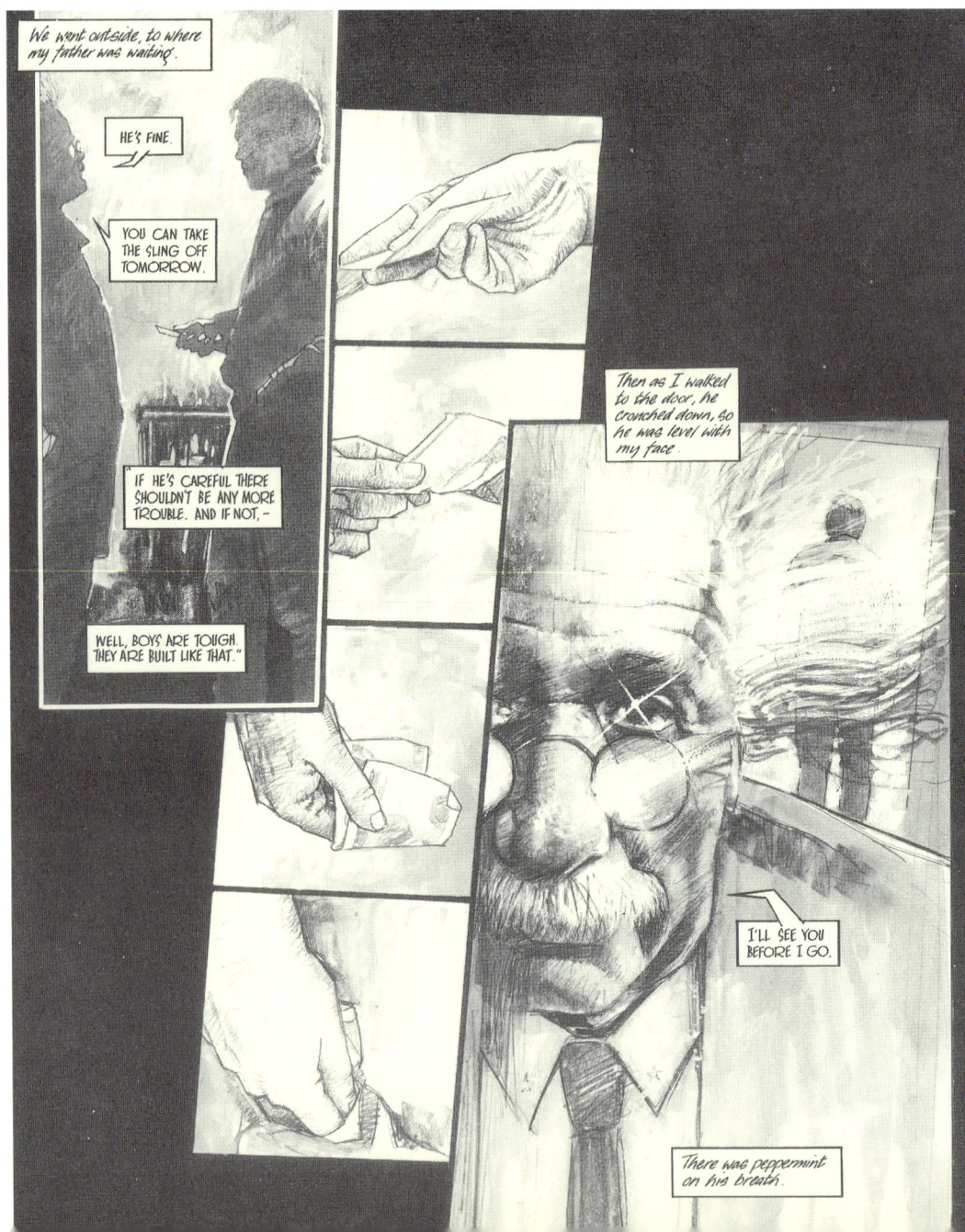

Page from
Violent Cases by
Neil Gaiman,
Dave McKean and
Alan Moore,
Titan Books, 1987

chiaroscuro
painting

'Christ is shown at the moment of blessing the bread and revealing his true identity to the disciples whom he met as they made their way to Emmaus. Looking at the painting, we are invited to participate in the drama across the fourth side of the table with Christ the only figure facing us. Caravaggio uses the receding table to help plot the space inside the picture. The disciples' arms confine the space at the side. Their motion helps draw us in. The foreshortened arm almost comes out of the picture. Details such as the basket of fruit are used to add tension: it almost falls off the table. Caravaggio's Christ is youthful and beardless. Probable influences for this come from Leonardo and Michelangelo's Christ from the Sistine Chapel.'

Notes taken from The National Gallery's CD–ROM: *Microsoft Art Gallery,* 1993

The Supper at Emmaus by Caravaggio, 1601 National Gallery, London

Look carefully at this painting and then discuss the questions on the right.

1 In our day-to-day life, we can understand a lot of what people say from reading the gestures they make while talking. In painting, these gestures are frozen, and we have to guess at what is being said and shown. What gestures are the three figures in *The Supper at Emmaus* making? How are they sitting or standing? What do you think these movements might mean? Do they tell us anything about these characters, for example who they are or what their relationship to each other might be?

2 How has Caravaggio placed these figures to shape and frame the picture?

3 Look at the characters' clothes and hair. How do these figures differ in appearance? What do these differences tell us about the figures and the overall story or meaning behind the painting?

4 What objects can you find in the picture? Explain how these objects might help us to understand what is happening in this scene.

film
noir

**Look carefully at this
film still and then discuss
the questions below:**

Film still from
The Blue Gardenia,
directed by Fritz
Lang, 1953

1 What mood does the lighting create?

2 What type of film do you think it belongs to? For example, is it a comedy?

3 What storyline does this image suggest? For example, what is likely to happen next? What has happened in the scene before?

the blue
gardenia

Film still from
The Blue Gardenia,
directed by Fritz Lang,
1953

the supper
at emmaus

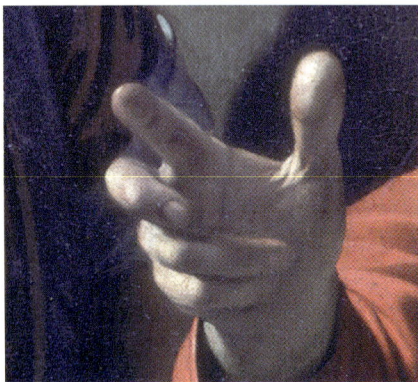

Top:
The Supper at Emmaus by
Caravaggio, 1601
National Gallery,
London,
details of which are
shown below

digital still life

Discuss the following questions while you watch Video Clips 1 and 2:

1 How has Le Grice managed to create a moving sequence using a still object?

2 How are the images sequenced? Do they follow a logical progression?

3 Does the film have a fixed point of view?

4 How can abstract work include objects and figures?

5 How does the music relate to the image sequences?

Film stills from
Digital Still Life,
images and video by
Malcolm le Grice,
1989

blank storyboard

Setting
environment and
atmosphere, props,
etc.

**Physical
description**
clothes, looks, action,
etc. of actor/actress

Camera shot
close-up, medium
shot, long shot, low
angle, high angle, etc.

**Camera
movement**
still, moving, etc.

**Sound effects
(SFX)**
special/background
sounds, etc.

Music
type and mood

Voice
who is speaking?
(write what is being
said in the Script
column)

Lighting
type of lighting
(i.e. where is it
coming from? is it
shining on one spot
or is it spread
diffusely?)

Setting

Physical description

Camera shot

Camera movement

Sound effects

Music

Voice

Lighting

SHOT NUMBER:

SCRIPT

Setting

Physical description

Camera shot

Camera movement

Sound effects

Music

Voice

Lighting

SHOT NUMBER:

SCRIPT

Setting

Physical description

Camera shot

Camera movement

Sound effects

Music

Voice

Lighting

SHOT NUMBER:

SCRIPT

illustrated
storyboard

SHOT 1

Setting
child's bedroom,
bunkbed, pillows,
duvets, two walls

**Physical
description**
Alice, seemingly
asleep

Camera shot
fade-in, MCU

**Camera
movement**
camera pans down

SHOT 2

**Physical
description**
we see nothing of
parents' faces, child
awake

**Camera
movement**
tilt down to bottom
bunk and track
around parents who
exit camera right.
Slight zoom on boy

SHOT 3

Setting
two walls, door,
lightswitch

**Physical
description**
back of mother and
father exiting

Camera shot
MS

SHOT 4

**Physical
description**
closing of door, light
gradually retreating
from room

Soundtrack
slow increase of
mysterious sounding
atmospheric music –
continues getting
louder and louder
throughout this
sequence

SHOT 5

**Physical
description**
door closed, only light
of keyhole can be
seen

Camera shot
CU

SHOT 6

**Physical
description**
boy watching parents
leave

Camera shot
MS

Sound effects
a noise

Script
'Did you hear that?'

MODULE **a** RESOURCES

SHOT 7

Setting
two walls, door, door knob, keyhole, light coming through key-hole and under door

Physical description
boy walking towards door

Camera shot
MCU

Sound effects
boy's footsteps, slight squeaking

SHOT 8

Physical description
boy approaching door and looking through keyhole

SHOT 9

Physical description
from the boy's point of view (POV) through the keyhole he can see the rest of the house

Camera shot
CU

SHOT 10

Physical description
boy sitting in front of the door, waiting

Camera movement
track round the boy to left then pan right to opposite corner

Lighting
Light under the door, and through the door keyhole

SHOT 11

Setting
corner of the children's bedroom

Physical description
toys, desk, chair

Camera shot
LS

Camera movement
slow track

SHOT 12

Physical description
on hearing noise boy looks startled

Camera shot
CU

Camera movement
deep shot shifting focus from boy's face to corner

Soundtrack
noise, like a drop of water followed by a slithering sound

SHOT 13

Setting
corner of a room with
door

**Physical
description**
boy turns round,
trying to make out
the noise

Camera shot
LS & low angle

Soundtrack
another noise

Lighting
dark except near
door

SHOT 14

**Physical
description**
vague outline of
something

Camera shot
BCU

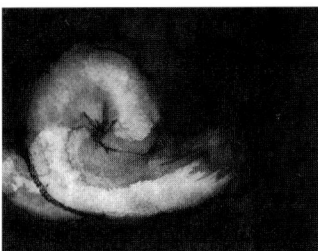

SHOT 15

**Physical
description**
boy watching corner,
anxious and turns
urgently to the door

Camera shot
CU

Soundtrack
muffled footsteps,
and voices from
outside the room

SHOT 16

**Physical
description**
cracks in door as
person walks past –
rays are blocked as
someone walks past

Camera shot
CU

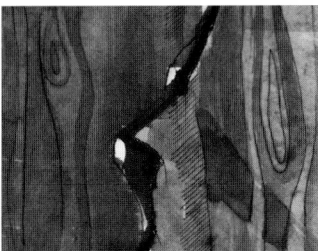

SHOT 17

**Physical
description**
hand trying to open
door handle but it
won't budge – he's
locked in

Camera shot
CU

Lighting
flood through
keyhole

SHOT 18

**Physical
description**
boy banging against
the door hopelessly,
trapped

Camera shot
LS & high angle –
fades out to black

Storyboard illustrated by Miguel Sapochnik, 1996

the art
of film design

In this Module, pupils explore the design aspects of film and how such elements as lighting, camera angles, music and sound effects can communicate meaning to a viewer. They also have the chance to create their own film-related publicity materials as part of a campaign.

Pupils are encouraged to develop their verbal interpretation of visual texts, to work from memory and to use their imagination. They are also able to extend their knowledge and understanding of influences and techniques by studying a wide range of illustrative material: film clips and stills, posters and prints. The module focuses in particular on expressionism and invites pupils to examine how expressionist conventions have been revived and reinterpreted over several decades in a range of art forms.

Summary

The module, which should take approximately fourteen weeks to complete (two hours per week), is divided into three parts:

Part 1 Reading the Film

Pupils are given the opportunity to analyse the basic elements of film narrative and *mise-en-scène* in a contemporary animation, *The Sandman*.

Activity 1.1:
Analysing *The Sandman*
120 minutes

Activity 1.2:
Telling Stories Through Moving Images
90 minutes

Activity 1.3:
Whose Point of View?
120 minutes

Part 2 Visual Influences

Pupils explore the connection between expressionism in fine art and expressionism in film, and examine how both have influenced the visual style of *The Sandman*.

Activity 2.1:
Looking Back and Looking Forward
120 minutes

Activity 2.2:
Drawing Comparisons
120 minutes

Activity 2.3:
Ideas for Set Design
120 minutes

Activity 2.4:
Scenescape
180 minutes

Part 3 Promoting the Film

Drawing on the illustrative material provided, as well as knowledge gained in Parts l and 2, pupils create an item of publicity material, to be used as part of a campaign.

Activity 3.1:
The Key Features of a Film Poster
120 minutes

Activity 3.2:
Targeting an Audience
120 minutes

Activity 3.3:
Creating Publicity Materials
(two parts):
120 minutes; 480 minutes

reading
the film

Objectives *In Part 1, pupils will*

▶ demonstrate their understanding of shot sizes and framing terms through drawing activities and sketchbook work

▶ develop their understanding of the elements of film narrative

Activity 1.1
analysing
The Sandman

National Curriculum reference
9b identify how visual elements are used to convey ideas, feelings and meanings in images and artefacts

Resources provided
Video Clip 3:
The Sandman by Colin Batty, Paul Berry and Ian Mackinnon, 1991
Video Clip 4:
Camera Angles in *The Sandman*
Video Clip 5:
Colours and Shadows in *The Sandman*
Activity Sheet 1.1:
The Sandman
Image Bank 1.1:
Film Stills from *The Sandman* (available as a separate card)
(Also, Information Sheet 1.2: Shot Sizes and Framing from Module A)

Resources required
Video player and monitor

Method
With the group, watch the whole of *The Sandman* (Video Clip 3) and allow time for all the emotive responses to emerge. The group may raise some interesting issues and ideas. For example: is the child a girl or a boy? What sort of clothes is he/she wearing? What is the exact relationship between the woman and the child? Does her manner appear to be unduly stern? The group might observe that there are no carpets in the house. What does this tell us?

Now use the questions on Activity Sheet 1.1: *The Sandman*, and Video

The Sandman: a modern expressionist animation, was first shown in 1992 on Channel 4 in the late evening, as part of a season of animations in a series called *Secret Passions*. The makers recognise that it may not be suitable for children under 9.

Clip 4: *The Sandman* – Camera Angles and Video Clip 5: *The Sandman* – Colours and Shadows to help pupils analyse and understand the film. Use Image Bank 1.1: Film Stills from *The Sandman* as a general aid to this activity.

Invite pupils to discuss the intentions of the film's makers. How effective are their techniques?

Camera angles
Pupils often devise their own terminology to describe camera angles and positions. Remind them of the recognised terms (Information Sheet 1.2: Shot Sizes and Framing from Module A). What are the merits of the recognised terms? How do they compare with pupils' own descriptions or labels?

Colours and shadows
When considering the use of colour and light in other films, discuss examples like *ET* (strong use of blue), *Empire of the Sun* (orange and red) and *The Last Emperor* (orange and red). What examples can the group come up with?

Sound
With the group, discuss how atmosphere is created through music and sound effects. Examine the synchronisation of visual movement with sounds and music in Video Clip 3. How does the sequence of images and sounds convey the stealth of *The Sandman*? What effects are created by the sound of the chiming clock and the movements of the woman and child?

Activity 1.2

telling stories through moving images

National Curriculum reference

8b select and record observations and ideas, and research and organise a range of visual evidence and information, using a sketchbook

Resources provided

Video Clip 3:
The Sandman

Resources required

Video player and monitor; sketchbooks; drawing materials

Method

First, ask pupils to write or draw their responses to *The Sandman* in their sketchbooks.

Play Video Clip 3 again and ask the group to identify the different elements of the film. Pupils may suggest any or all of the following: colours, camera angles, music, sound effects, props, characterisation, expression and movements, lighting. Which ingredients help to create atmosphere and emotion? How do they achieve their effect?

Brainstorm the different responses and write them on the board for all to share.

Working individually or in pairs, pupils should now compose a poem or short piece of prose telling the story of *The Sandman* as viewed. (They should be encouraged to use film language and technical terms wherever possible.) Pupils may wish to use illustrations from their sketchbooks to accompany their written texts.

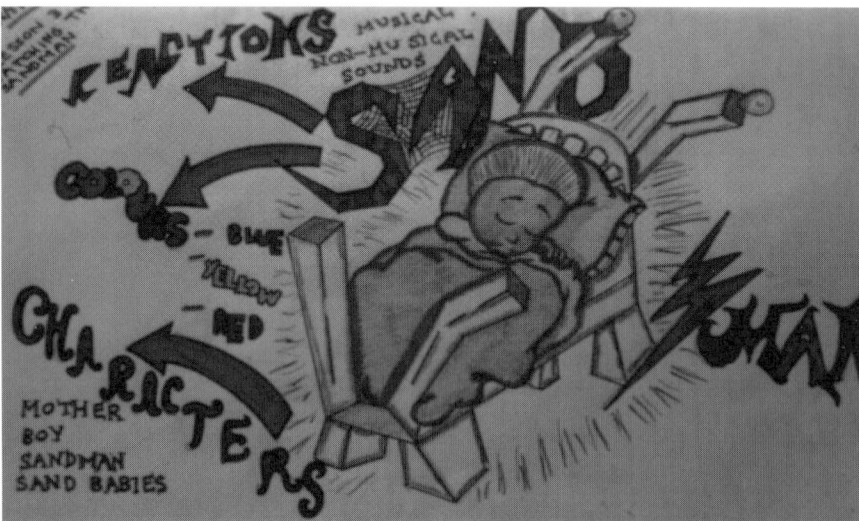

Example of a pupil's sketchbook work.
Ria Chantler, Ifield Community College

Activity 1.3
whose point of view?

National Curriculum reference
8c experiment with and select from visual and other source material to stimulate and develop ideas for independent work

Resources provided
Video Clip 3:
The Sandman

Resources required
Video player and monitor; sketchbooks; drawing materials

Method
Organise pupils into groups and ask them to do one or more of the following:

1 Write up or retell to a partner a short sequence from *The Sandman*, describing the events as witnessed by one of the characters.

2 In a sketchbook, draw two or three shots of the stairs as shown in *The Sandman*, from the perspective of the child. (Remind pupils to consider shot sizes and framing.)

3 Choose three distinctive images from *The Sandman* and draw them into a sketchbook for future reference. One image must show a character; another must show a prop. (Encourage pupils to frame their images in cinema-screen-shaped boxes.)

visual
influences

Objectives *In Part 2, pupils will*

▶ study a style or period of art in its historical context

▶ investigate, through practical work, the influence of one art form on another

▶ record visual information for use in later work

Activity 2.1
looking back and looking forward

National Curriculum reference
9c relate art, craft and design to its social, historical and cultural context, e.g. identify codes and conventions used in different times and cultures

Resources provided
Activity Sheet 2.1:
German Expressionist Prints

Resources required
Sketchbooks; drawing materials

Method
With the group, discuss Activity Sheet 2.1: German Expressionist Prints, using the questions as a guide. Explore the group's responses to the images. In particular, examine how distortion creates atmosphere, and expresses and elicits emotion.

Now ask pupils to copy parts of these images into their sketchbooks. They should then attempt to draw people and everyday objects in their sketchbooks in the same manner, recreating the expressionist style for themselves. (These drawings will be needed in later activities.)

Expressionism
Introduce as much or as little detail about the idea of expressionism as you see fit. Most books on the subject mention the difficulty of defining the concept, and many of the key figures associated with its distinctive style preferred not to be labelled as part of a movement!

In *Expressionism* (World University Library, Weidenfeld and Nicolson, 1970), John Willett states:

'Expressionism is normally:

1 a family characteristic of modern Germanic art, literature, music and theatre, from the turn of the century to the present day

2 a particular modern German movement which lasted roughly between 1910 and 1922

3 a quality of expressive emphasis and distortion which may be found in the works of art of any people or period'

The aim of this particular activity is to explore the formal stylistic aspects of distortion and deep emotion. Activity Sheet 2.1 shows prints produced in Germany in the period 1902–22. The influence of such images on design and film is evident in the *The Cabinet of Dr Caligari* (see Activity 2.2).

Sketchbook image in expressionist style, Holy Cross School

Activity 2.2
drawing comparisons

National Curriculum reference
9a recognise the diverse methods and approaches used by artists, craftspeople and designers

Resources provided
Video Clip 3:
The Sandman (from the beginning of the sequence when the Sandman enters the house)
Video Clip 7:
Excerpt from *The Cabinet of Dr Caligari* by Robert Wiene, 1919
Video Clip 6:
The Sandman
The producers talk about its making
Activity Sheet 2.2:
Drawing Comparisons
Information Sheet 2.1:
The Sandman and *The Cabinet of Dr Caligari*

Resources required
Video player and monitor

Method
With the group, watch Video Clip 7 and encourage pupils to voice their thoughts and opinions.

Then rewatch *The Sandman* (from the sequence where the Sandman enters the house) and, using the questions and table on Activity Sheet 2.2, invite pupils to compare and contrast the two sequences as part of a group discussion.

Draw attention to the different elements that contribute towards the overall effect: lighting, props, sets, characters, costumes, make-up, facial expressions, gestures. Encourage pupils to comment on the use of colour versus black and white, the choice of characters and the choice of story/subject matter. For example, both films feature a fear of the unknown as a common theme.

Now watch and discuss Video Clip 6 to find out how the makers of *The Sandman* were influenced by such films as *The Cabinet of Dr Caligari*.

Intended Audience
The questions on Activity Sheet 2.2 about the intended audience are designed to explore pupils' assumptions and to enable the group to consider the wider topic of 'an audience' for any medium or work or art.

If you wish to talk through the differences/similarities, let the group see Information Sheet 2.1. However, the aim of this activity is not so much to test knowledge as to explore pupils' judgements and opinions. For example, does the technique of animation presuppose an audience of children? If so, how young should the children be? Does melodrama and black and white film imply an exclusively adult or middle-aged viewer? Make sure pupils are aware of the reasons behind their judgements, if only to help them question them further.

Background Notes on *The Cabinet of Dr Caligari*
This German film, dating from 1919, was produced by Erich Pommer and directed by Robert Wiene. The authors of the story, Carl Mayer and Hans Janowitz, had a particular audience in mind and a particular message to convey when they devised the tale of the evil Dr Caligari and his slave, Cesar.

There was a revolutionary mood abroad in post-World War I Germany, and Janowitz and Mayer believed that their hatred of the rigid autocracy of the day could best be expressed on screen. By transferring the story to film and by using the most modern techniques available, they were able to create nightmarish images, elicit strong emotions and so intensify the impact of the allegory.

Dr Caligari symbolised an unlimited authority, using power to satisfy his lust for domination, and ruthlessly violating all human rights and values. The whole film is riddled with symbolism. For example, the town clerk sits on an enormous swivel chair; a vast, almost never-ending staircase leads to Dr Caligari's office. Both these images reinforce the feeling of the state's power and superiority.

The film, which caused shock and outrage wherever it was shown, was intended for an adult audience who were looking for serious issues and ideas when they visited the cinema. It should be remembered that the majority of the cinema-going public of the time enjoyed the usual fare of melodramas and comedies.

Video Clip 7 shows Cesar, who is sent out by Dr Caligari on nocturnal killing journeys. Cesar is sleepwalking and unaware of what he is doing.

Activity 2.3

ideas for set design

National Curriculum reference

9d identify how and why styles and traditions change over time and from place to place, recognising the contribution of artists, craftspeople and designers

Resources provided

Video Clip 7:
Excerpt from *The Cabinet of Dr Caligari*
Information Sheet 2.2:
Expressionism in Film

Resources needed

Video player and monitor; sketchbooks; drawing materials (including charcoal, Indian ink, hard and soft pencils)

Method

With the group, watch Video Clip 7 again and this time discuss the angled sets, the costumes and the make-up. Then look at Information Sheet 2.2. Ask pupils to make drawings of a window, door, stair or chair in their sketchbooks using expressionist conventions. Pupils should experiment with the drawing materials mentioned above. They may refer to these if they elect to make model sets as part of Activity 3.3.

Expressionist door. Josie-May Ballard, Ifield Community College

Activity 2.4

scenescape

National Curriculum reference

8c experiment with and select from visual and other source material to stimulate and develop ideas for independent work

Resources provided

Video Clip 3:
The Sandman
Video Clip 8:
Extract from the opening to *Metropolis* by Fritz Lang, 1926
Video Clip 9:
From the opening to *Blade Runner* by Ridley Scott, 1982
Video Clip 10:
The City by Carole Bellon and Bella Kerr, 1991
Activity Sheet 2.3:
Graphic Illustrators

Resources required

Video player and monitor; sketchbooks, drawing materials

Select and record a few opening sequences from films/videos/television programmes that depict city scenes or other landscapes. Several television soap operas use this device – beginning with an aerial shot and gradually leading the viewer down to street level. In the famous film *Casablanca*, the viewer is shown a map of Africa before being drawn down into the streets of the town. Such a descent is usually achieved by means of a series of dissolves or seamlessly edited shots.

Method

Divide the pupils into small groups and rotate them through the following exercises.

1 Opening sequences

Pupils should watch the opening sequences to two or three films or soap operas, and comment on what they see, using these questions as a guide:

▶ How do these sequences set the scene for what is to follow?
▶ How do they create a sense of place, space and atmosphere?
▶ How much of each sequence simply films what you might expect to see in a town or village, for example the actual streets and buildings of Liverpool or the East End of London?
▶ How much of each sequence focuses on models and life-size three-dimensional sets (think, for example, of *Blade Runner, 2001*)?
▶ What special effects have been added and what do they contribute to the atmosphere (think, for example, of the aeronautics at the start of the *Superman* and *Batman* films)?
▶ Consider how these scenes may have started life as a series of single images, detailed background drawings of landscapes or towns, in a designer's sketchbook.

Pupils should then select one of the opening sequences they have viewed and sketch it out in a rough series of drawings, starting from the air and finishing at ground level, making notes as they go on camera movements and angles, and how the transition from one level or viewpoint to another can be achieved by mixing and cutting.

2 The graphic illustrator
This part of the activity looks again at distortion and examines how the work of illustrators and artists can be affected by any number of outside influences. The exercise also serves to remind pupils just how dark and macabre traditional fairy tales can be. The makers of *The Sandman*, when describing their film, point out that the usual parental blessing given to a child at bedtime would have been

'the Sandman sprinkles sand into the eyes of children to help them sleep'

which the Brothers Grimm transformed into the far more gothic

'and the Sandman robs the eyes of children if they don't sleep'

Ask pupils to look at Activity Sheet 2.3.

Image 1 is an illustration from a children's book of fairy tales by Arthur Rackham. Image 2 is by the Swedish artist and illustrator Gustaf Tenggren. Tenggren worked at the Disney studio during the late 1930s and this particular image is an 'inspirational painting' prepared for *Pinocchio* (1940).

It is interesting to learn that Tenggren:

'greatly admired the work of Arthur Rackham and also absorbed ideas from films, noting in particular the influence of Hollywood on commercial art, with its suggestions of different camera angles and movement.'
Robin Allan from *Art into Film* (supplement in *Sight and Sound*, 1994)

In the same supplement, Robin Allan describes the content and style of these two images in more detail:

'Grotesque and fantastic [image 1], this drawing demonstrates the linear facility which endeared Rackham to Disney and his colleagues. The old woman is benign, but could easily become the terrifying witch familiar to us from Disney; the cat has malignity that allies it to the old woman, while Rackham's famous gnarled trees appear malevolent even when not actually transmogrified into tortured limbs and faces…

…The angle of shot [image 2] and the rich detailing of the foreground and rooftop – from the tiling on the gables to the weather vane and bird's nest – are precisely matched in the final-artwork of the film. The fox, cat and Pinocchio come into frame on the left and then parade up the street in the 'Hi Diddle De Dee' music number, going round the centrally placed tree and then off right…. note the altogether false perspective of the overhead shot which shows Tenggren's absorption of cinema into his visual perception.'
Robin Allan (ibid.)

With the pupils, discuss the questions provided. How similar are the two images? How have the artists used distortion, colour and perspective? How have they managed to blend the central figures into the background?

Once the discussion is over, pupils should draw one large scene from a famous fairy tale, using distortion and unusual perspectives. (It may help to remind them of the distorted sets featured in *The Sandman*.) The finished scenes could become the basis for a simple animated film.

3 Bringing the scene to life
Pupils should watch Video Clip 10: *The City*. This demonstrates how a three-dimensional model made from quite basic materials can be used to create the illusion of a city.

Ask pupils to consider how lighting and sound also contribute to the overall atmosphere of the clip.

They should then make the rough sketches necessary to build a total landscape, seascape or skyline, and consider how they would introduce key features, such as tower blocks or underwater scenery, etc., using two- or three-dimensional models. (It is interesting to note that the model for *Blade Runner*'s skyscape was not much more than three metres wide, so there is much that can be achieved on a modest budget – if one eliminates the special effects.)

The City was made for BBC2 by new film makers who were given one minute only in which to express their ideas.

promoting
the film

Objectives *In Part 3, pupils will*

▶ discuss the function of publicity material

▶ examine the likely audience for a particular film

▶ use sketchbook studies prepared in earlier activities to create an item of publicity material for *The Sandman*

Activity 3.1

the key features of a film poster

National Curriculum reference
9e express ideas and opinions and justify preferences, using knowledge and an art, craft and design vocabulary

Resources provided
Activity Sheet 3.1:
The Key Features of a Film Poster

Method
With the group, discuss the *Blade Runner* poster on Activity Sheet 3.1 using the questions provided.

This exercise should generate comments on genre and audience which will lead the group into the next activity.

Activity 3.2

targeting an audience

National Curriculum reference
8e Select from and interpret visual elements and realise their intentions in a range of media

Resources provided
Activity Sheet 3.2:
Words and Images
Image Bank 3.1:
Early Twentieth-Century Film Posters
Image Bank 3.2:
Modern Film Posters
Image Bank 3.3:
A Billboard Poster

Method
Work through Activity Sheet 3.2: Words and Images with the group, using the questions and table provided. Help pupils understand how poster designers use and adapt the following in order to attract different audiences and to indicate genre (western, sci-fi, Manga):

▶ language
▶ lettering/typeface
▶ layout/design
▶ images
▶ colour

The content and style of a poster will usually suggest the genre of the film.

Compare the two posters for *Metropolis*, in their 1926 and 1985 versions (Image Bank 3.1).

How have film posters changed over the years? It is interesting to note for example, that stars and personalities feature far more prominently today than they did in the past. Films in the 1990s are 'star-led'.

Activity 3.3

creating publicity materials

National Curriculum reference

8d Select from and experiment with materials, images and ideas, and extend their knowledge and experience of a range of materials, tools and techniques

Resources provided

Video Clip 3: *The Sandman*
Video Clip 8: Excerpt from *The Cabinet of Dr Caligari*
Video Clip 9:
From the opening to *Blade Runner*
Activity Sheet 3.1:
The Key Features of a Film Poster
Activity Sheet 3.2:
Words and Images
Activity Sheet 3.3:
Promoting *The Sandman*
Image Bank 3.1:
Early Twentieth-Century Film Posters
Image Bank 3.2:
Modern Film Posters
Image Bank 3.3:
A Billboard Poster
Video Gallery (Module B)

Resources required

Video player and monitor; sketchbooks, drawing materials; work completed in Parts 1 and 2.

It would be an advantage to collect a range of film posters covering different genres and to allow the group to watch a selection of promotional trailers.

Refer to the section on Technical Guidance (p.70) for a discussion of appropriate technical equipment.

Method

This activity is divided into two parts. The first should take approximately 120 minutes and the second about 480 minutes. Both parts of the activity revolve around one objective: to create a piece of promotional material for *The Sandman*.

Give the pupils the brief on Activity Sheet 3.3. Tell the whole group that there is to be a festival celebrating British animation and *The Sandman* has been chosen as the lead film. Pupils have to create a poster, a model set or a trailer to publicise the film.

You may wish to divide the pupils into smaller groups and to allocate a different project to each one. In this way, the class will be able to assess a spectrum of materials and see how *The Sandman* has been marketed to a variety of specific audiences.

1 Choosing the image
In this part of the activity, pupils make preparatory sketches for their poster, model set or trailer. They should examine Activity Sheet 3.3 carefully and be aware of factors such as audience and location before proceeding.

Show Video Clip 3 again and ask pupils to discuss which images from *The Sandman* they would select in order to promote the film. What key design elements would they feature most prominently? Which scenes convey a sense of the style of the film? Which scenes would give a taste of the plot?

Ask each group to sketch out and experiment with possible images, both background and foreground.

Film poster for
The Sandman.
Christopher
Lashwood, James
Smyth and Ryan
Corbett, Holy Cross
School

Pupils may find it helpful to look
again at the models/sets used in the
opening to *Blade Runner* and the
excerpt from *The Cabinet of Dr
Caligari.*

2 Targeting an audience

Pupils can now proceed with their
posters, model sets and trailers. They
can use all the sketchbook material
they have prepared so far in the
module, as well as the film itself and
all the other resources provided here.

Creating a poster

Those who choose to create a poster
will need to consider an appropriate
size and scale, bearing in mind the
context and the target audience.
For example, billboard posters (to be
viewed by drivers and travellers) are
usually landscape-shaped, whereas
posters used in bus shelters (to be
viewed by pedestrians) are usually
smaller and portrait-shaped.
A smaller version of the poster
(featuring critics' quotes) may be
used in newspapers and magazines.

Pupils will also need to think about
the following:

▶ For how long will the poster be
displayed?
▶ Should they use the whole of a
key image from the film, or just part?
▶ What typeface should they use to
indicate *The Sandman*'s genre?
▶ What written information and
credits should they include?

Encourage the group to experiment
with a range of materials, ideas and
processes – charcoal and erasers;
black ink and bleach; wax-resist
techniques; watercolour? Typed or
written text could be incorporated
into an image or used as a pattern.
You can either photocopy the images
from Image Bank 1.1: Film stills
from *The Sandman* or scan them
into a computer.

Creating a film trailer

Those who choose to create a trailer
will need additional equipment.
They will need to have the facility to
transfer clips from one video tape to
another, and to dub on one or more
soundtracks. This can be done
reasonably effectively using two
video recorders, and a microphone
input on one of the video cassette
recorders or cameras.

Pupils should select the shots they
wish to use in their trailer from *The
Sandman* film itself, from artwork
and from images they have drawn in
their own sketchbooks.

They should think carefully why
they have selected particular shots
and also about the target audience.
Where will the trailer be shown?
On television or at the cinema?

Model set for
The Sandman.
Anthony Doyle,
Darion Farlo,
Holy Cross School

Creating a model set

Those who choose to create a model set will need to consider the appropriate size and scale, bearing in mind its function and purpose. Pupils should be briefed to produce it as though for a director, or as a prop for a pre-release event in the cinema foyer. Use lights and shadows to enhance the atmosphere and dramatic effect. Simple card and textiles can be used to great effect.

The stills on videotape Video Gallery (Module B) show pupils working on sets and posters.

Pupils should revisit Activity 2.4: Ideas for Set Design, reread their sketchbook notes and perhaps rewatch Video Clip 10: *The City*, which uses very simple materials to suggest the subterranean and cityscapes.

Once they have selected their shots, pupils will need to decide on the accompanying music, voice-over and background sounds/sound effects they want to use. They need to consider the following:

▶ Does the script for the voice-over need to hold the viewer's attention throughout the trailer, or should the film speak for itself, with minimal aural intervention?
▶ What linking shots do they want to include?
▶ How should they begin and end the trailer? With still or moving images? A still showing just the title of the film is a conventional way of ending a trailer.

They could test out their ideas by drawing a storyboard (see Activity 2.2 in Module A) and/or by showing a rough version to the rest of the class. They could record the reactions of their fellow pupils and modify the trailer in the light of these responses.

Evaluation

Once all the materials have been completed, pupils should review each other's work. How effective is each piece in terms of design? Has each group fulfilled the criteria given in the brief?

These may be summarised as follows:

▶ target audience
▶ location
▶ format information/credits
▶ peer group response and modifications.

assessment
table

Learning outcomes	Activities	Evidence	Assessment methods
Select from a range of stills from *The Sandman*; propose design solutions to set briefs in sketchbooks	Part 3: Activities 3.3	Visual research and written notes in sketchbook	Observation; evaluation of sketchbook
Identify and discuss the visual elements of *The Sandman* and make a visual representation of the film's language	Part 1: Activities 1.1, 1.2	Illustration; oral work	Question and discussion
Consider size and scale, and how to show the importance of certain characteristics in the poster and promotional trailer	Part 3: Activities 3.1, 3.3	Sketchbook, containing experiments with processes, written text and compositions	Evaluation of product(s)
Express opinions about the way reality is distorted in *The Sandman* and German expressionist resources provided; make sketches	Part 2: Activity 2.1	Sketchbook; loose design sheets, showing image and text samples	Question and discussion; evaluation of sketchbook
Compare the German expressionist resources and *The Sandman*, recognising period as well as technological similarities and differences	Part 2: Activity 2.2	Visual and written notes in sketchbook, showing sketches of distortions of *The Sandman* sets and characters	Question and discussion
Identify contribution of artists in construction of film set design and *mise-en-scène*	Part 2 Activity 2.3	Visual research and drawings in sketchbooks	Observation; evaluation of sketchbook
Study, experiment with and select visual material from contemporary film and television makers and twentieth-century illustrators	Part 2 Activity 2.4	Visual and written notes in the sketchbook; oral discussion	Observation; evaluation of sketchbook
Specify the audience and where they would be likely to see material	Part 3: Activity 3.3	Oral discussion; written notes	Observation; evaluation of sketchbook
Invite responses to the design work from real audiences in school and at home; discuss the effectiveness of the products	Part 3: Activity 3.3	Poster, set, trailer; oral discussion; pupil self-assessment	Observation; evaluation of product(s)

The Sandman

camera angles

**Look carefully at
Video Clip 4: *The Sandman*
– Camera Angles,
then answer these questions:**

1 Write down the names of three different camera angles or framing used in these images. Describe the setting briefly. (Use Information Sheet 1.2: Shot Sizes and Framing from Module A to help you.)

2 Can you say where the camera has been placed in each image? Is it to the left, to the right, above or below the subject?

3 Can you find an example of:

▶ a close-up (CU)
▶ a big close-up (BCU)
▶ a mid shot (MS)
▶ a long shot (LS)?

colours and shadows

**Look carefully at
Video Clip 5: *The Sandman*
– Colours and Shadows,
then answer these questions:**

1 What is the main colour used in each of these images?

2 What does this colour mean to you? Does this colour affect the way you think about or understand the film? If so, how?

3 What do the colours yellow and orange mean to you? Do you link them with particular feelings?

4 What other strong colours are used in *The Sandman*? What do they suggest to you?

5 Can you name some other films that use one or two strong colours in a striking and effective way?

6 Describe the sequences where shadows are very noticeable; what effect do these shadows create? Explain how the shots must have been set up for lighting.

sound

Now watch Video Clip 3 and make a list of all the sound effects and music you can hear. In each case, how does what you hear match up to what you see? What kind of atmosphere does each sound create?

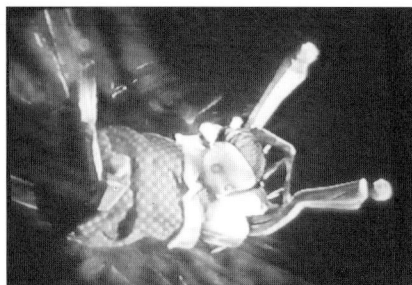

Still from
The Sandman of child
in bed, high angle,
tilted shot

Still from
The Sandman of
mother in close up

German expressionist prints

1 Look closely at these four prints and then

▶ describe what is in each image (the content)
▶ comment on the way the artists distort the people and objects in each image (the form)

2 How realistic are these images? What atmosphere do they create? How do they make you feel?

3 Can you think of some images from *The Sandman* which look similar to these prints?

4 Draw parts of these prints into your sketchbook for future reference.

Above:
Print of woodcut,
Elizabeth-Bridge,
Ernst Ludwig
Kirchner, 1912

Above right:
Print of woodcut,
Cityscape from Soest,
Schmidt Rotluff,
1923

Right:
Print of woodcut,
'*The Cry*, Karl Jakob
Hirsch, 1920

Far right:
Print of woodcut,
*Give us our Daily
Bread*, Max
Pechstein, 1923

drawing
comparisons

Compare and contrast the clips from *The Sandman* and *The Cabinet of Dr Caligari* by writing and drawing your answers to the questions below. You may find it helpful to copy the table into your sketchbook and fill it in while you are watching the two excerpts.

1 Describe the camera's position and angle in each clip. How often does the camera position change in each excerpt?

2 Think of the distorted props and sets used in the two clips. How similar are they?

3 Think who these films were made for and who might be interested in watching them. How old would they be? Would they be male or female? What type of people would they be? Would the same type of person be interested in both films?

Top:
English modern expressionist animation.
Still from
The Sandman
Batty, Berry and Mackinnon

Bottom:
German expressionist film.
Still from *The Cabinet of Dr Caligari*
Designers: Hermann Warm, Walter Rohnig and Walter Reimann

Elements	The Sandman	The Cabinet of Dr Caligari
Camera movement		
Camera angle		
Camera perspective		
Sets		
Props		
Character types		
Facial expressions		
Clothes		
Make-up		
Lighting		

The Sandman
and The Cabinet of Dr Caligari

Differences

The main differences are technological.

▶ In *The Sandman*, the camera roves around and looks at the subject from above or below; in *The Cabinet of Dr Caligari*, the camera is fixed.

▶ *The Cabinet of Dr Caligari* features actors. Most of the sets and props, however, are two-dimensional and painted on to canvas. All the characters in *The Sandman* are static models which have to be animated by still-frame control. This technique creates jerky movements.

Similarities

▶ Both films create a mood of fear and uncertainty.
▶ Both feature a character who is frightened and a character who is frightening.
▶ Both excerpts are set in a bedroom, a place where one is likely to experience a nightmare.
▶ Both feature distorted scenery and dark shadows.
▶ Close-ups, particularly of the characters' eyes, play an important part in conveying emotion and atmosphere.

Audience

The Sandman was made in England in 1991. It was designed for both adults and children (over nine years old) and was first shown on Channel 4 in the late evening as part of a series of animations in a series called *Secret Passions*. The film was also designed to be shown in the cinema.

The Cabinet of Dr Caligari was made in Germany in 1919 and was intended for a minority adult audience. Such people went to the cinema to see artistically satisfying films which contained serious and often nightmarish ideas and messages. The majority of the public at the time, however, preferred comedies and melodramas.

Still from
The Sandman

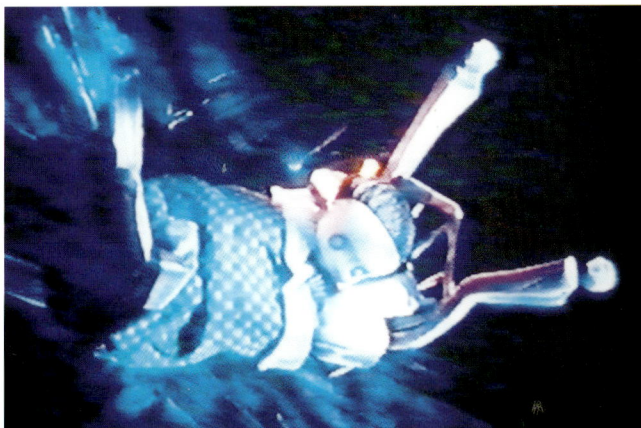

Still from
*The Cabinet of
Dr Caligari*

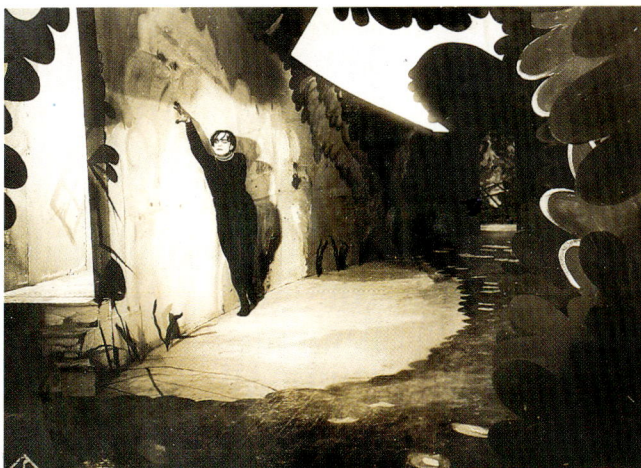

graphic illustrators

Look carefully at these images and then answer the following questions:

1 How realistic are these drawings?

2 How do they make you feel? How have the illustrators created that feeling?

3 Draw a detailed background setting of your own to illustrate a scene from a well-known fairy tale, such as *Little Red Riding Hood*, *The Three Little Pigs*, *Hansel and Gretel*, *Anansi*. Try to use distortion and to draw buildings and trees from unusual angles.

Painting by Gustaf Tenggren for the Walt Disney *Pinocchio* animation, 1940

Illustration by Arthur Rackham from his book of fairy tales called *Mother Goose*, 1913

expressionism
in film

The Cabinet of Dr Caligari was designed by Hermann Warm, Walter Rorhrig and Walter Reimann. They managed to create some interesting effects using very cheap and simple materials. (Most of the sets, props and backdrops were made from painted canvas.) Nothing before the camera looks realistic: the angular houses lean over, the ground is coated in painted shapes and the windows are shaped like kites. All the actors wear heavy and exaggerated make-up which serves to distort their features. The film has been described as 'the cinema's first great nightmare' and the designers have certainly contributed to the atmosphere of fear and fantasy.

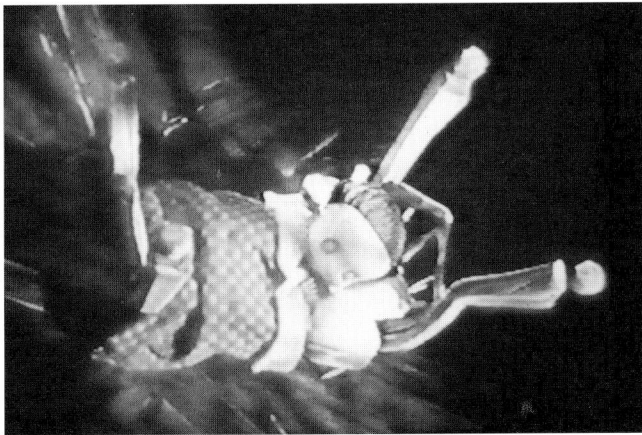

Top:
Stills from
*The Cabinet of
Dr Caligari*

Bottom:
Stills from
The Sandman

the key features
of a film poster

Study the film poster below and then answer the questions.

Images

1 What are the main images shown in the poster? Why do you think these have been selected?

2 How are these images positioned and 'blended?

3 How is colour used?

4 How is perspective used?

5 What type of film is *Blade Runner?* What genre does it belong to?

6 What characters do you think might feature in the film?

7 What do you think the story-line might be?

Written information

1 What type of information is usually given on a film poster?

2 Where is the information usually placed in relation to the images?

3 Look at these pieces of information on the *Blade Runner* poster:

▶ the names of the stars
▶ the title of the film
▶ the name of the director
▶ the name of the producer
▶ the name of the distributor
▶ the music/composer
▶ other credits

How are these treated in terms of size, shape, typeface?

4 Comment on the slogan used. Can you think of ways in which other films are described?

Film poster for
Blade Runner,
Ridley Scott, 1982

early twentieth-century film
posters

Above:
Film poster for
Metropolis,
Fritz Lang, 1926

Below:
Film poster for
Metropolis,
Fritz Lang, 1926.
The modern poster
design is for
Georgio Moroder's
1985 soundtrack
version of the film.

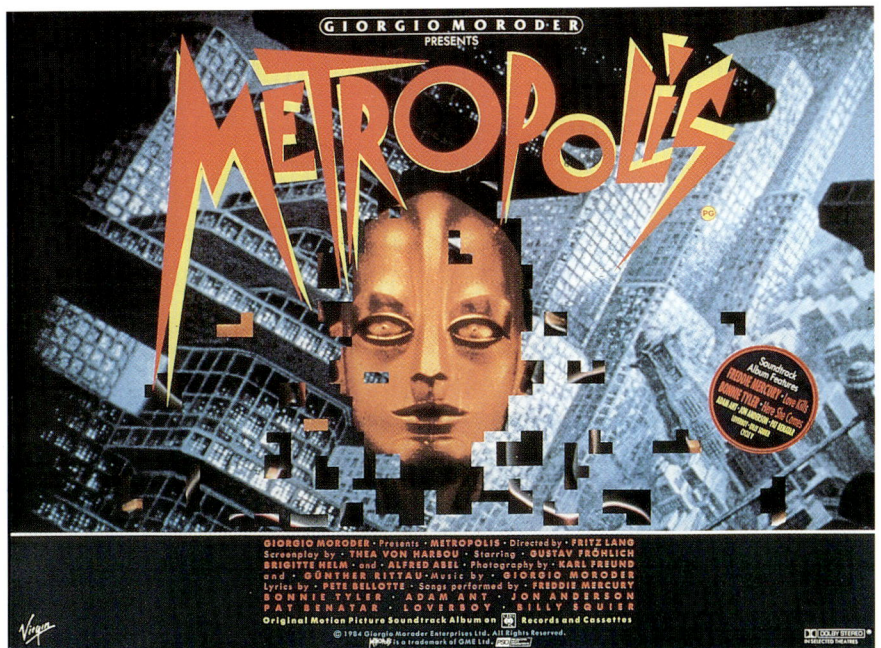

words
and images

Study the film posters on Activity Sheet 3.1 and Image Banks 3.1 and 3.2 and then answer the questions below. You may find it helpful to copy the table into your sketchbook and to make notes about each question while you are looking at the posters.

1 Who do you think each poster might appeal to? Can you give reasons for your answers?

2 Can you name the genre that each film belongs to (e.g. science fiction, comedy)?

3 Some of the films featured here may belong to more than one genre.

Is this clear from the posters?

4 Would some of these posters appeal more to women than men? Would some appeal more to men than women? If so, why? Would any appeal to both men and women?

5 What do the title and typeface on each poster tell you about the content of the film?

6 Have film poster designs changed over the years? If so, how?

7 Why do you think the poster advertising *Grease* was redrawn and handpainted for a Thai audience?

Film	Q1	Q2	Q3	Q4	Q5	Q6
Metropolis 1926						
Metropolis 1985						
Blade Runner						
The Odd Man Out						
Devil in a Blue Dress						
Last of the Mohicans						
Cyrano de Bergerac						
Grease						

promoting
The Sandman

The brief

You have been asked to design a poster, a 15-second trailer, or a model set to promote *The Sandman*.

Creating a poster

Before you begin, think about these points:

▶ Where will your poster be displayed? On a cinema wall, on a billboard or in a magazine?

▶ Who is it for? Adults, children or families?

▶ What information will you need to include on your poster and how will you present that information? (Look at Activity Sheets 3.1 and 3.2.)

▶ What materials and equipment will you need?

The credits

The credits you need to include in your poster are given below:

A Batty, Berry, McKinnon production, 1991

with the assistance of Cosgrove Productions

Puppets and sets
Colin Batty
Ian Mackinnon
Richard Sykes

Lighting Camera
Joe Dembinski

Rostrum Camera
Peter Kidd

Editor
Therese Lynch

Dubbing Mixer
John Wood

Music
Colin Towns

Animation and Direction
Paul Berry

Distributed by Vector Television

Creating a trailer

Make a 15-second trailer which must include *The Sandman*'s main characters: the Sandman and the child. Before you begin, think about the following:

▶ Where will it be shown? At a local major cinema? On television? In a small, special cinema for 'art' films?

▶ Who is it for? Adults, children or families?

▶ What information will you need to show in the trailer? What information can be spoken as a voice-over?

▶ How will you entice people to come and watch the film?

You can use all the materials and sketchbook work you have already collected.

Creating a model set

Your model set is to be used before the film is released or maybe even made. Before you begin, think about these points:

▶ Where will the model set be displayed? In a cinema foyer? Is it to be photographed and featured in a magazine article? Is it to be presented to the film director?

▶ Who is it for? Adults, children or families?

▶ What materials and equipment do you need?

(Look at Information Sheet 2.2: Expressionism in Film and Video Clip 10: *The City*.)

modern
film posters

Top:
Film poster for
The Odd Man Out,
Carol Reed, 1946

Middle left:
Film poster for
Devil in a Blue Dress,
Carl Franklin, 1996

Middle right:
Film poster for
Last of the Mohicans,
Michael Mann, 1992

Bottom:
Film poster for
Cyrano de Bergerac,
Jean-Paul
Rappaneau, 1990

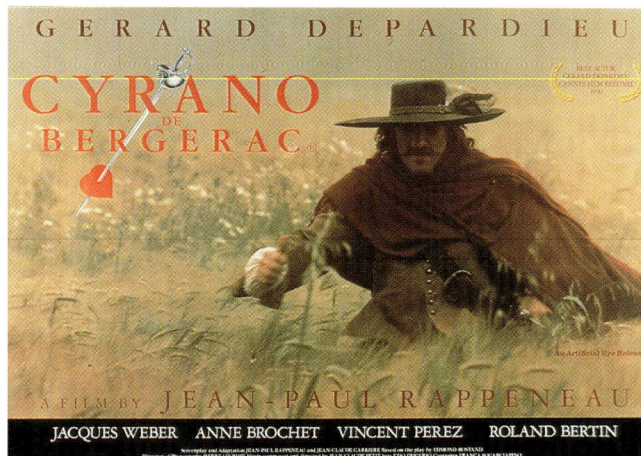

a billboard
poster

Billboard poster
for *Grease*, directed
by Randal Kleiner,
1978, Thailand

^aquestion
of identity

The aim of this module is to offer pupils the opportunity to analyse a range of television 'idents' (the short films between programmes that identify and brand the channel), to understand how and why they are made, and to go on to create idents and logos for themselves.

The activities encourage pupils to borrow ideas from fine art, television and film and to use a selection of materials when making their films. As in Modules A and B, sketchbook work plays an important part in the creative process.

By the end of the module, pupils will have demonstrated their ability to transform still images into moving sequences (accompanied by a synchronised soundtrack, if resources allow). They should also be able to show their understanding of product branding and the importance of targeting an audience.

Technical advice about the equipment needed for this module (and Modules A and B) is given on p.70.

Summary

The module, which should take a minimum of nine and a half weeks to complete (two hours per week, allowing time for evaluation), is divided into three parts:

Part 1 What are Television Idents?

Pupils analyse a selection of television idents, making judgements about their purpose and how they might fit into a programming schedule.

Activity 1.1:
Identifying Channels
120 minutes

Activity 1.2:
Into the Schedule
120 minutes

Part 2 Creating a Channel Identity

Pupils devise a new logo for a television channel and plan how they will use this as the basis for a short ident film. They also experiment with techniques and materials in 2-D and 3-D, and examine how the makers of idents have borrowed ideas from the fine arts.

Activity 2.1:
Logos: Size, Shape and Style
120 minutes

Activity 2.2:
Recycling Art Images
60 minutes

Activity 2.3:
Inventing a New Logo and Ident
120 minutes

Activity 2.4:
2-D to 3-D
120 minutes

Part 3 Producing a Television Channel Ident

Using the preparatory materials created in Parts 1 and 2, pupils produce short ident films. They then present their ideas to an audience and evaluate the response.

Activity 3.1:
Producing the Ident
360 minutes

Activity 3.2:
Presentation, Review and Modification
120 minutes

what are television idents

Objectives *In Part 1, pupils will*

▶ recognise and define television idents
▶ analyse and distinguish between different types of idents, understanding them as an art form

▶ begin to learn about the function of channel 'branding' by studying television conventions, genres and scheduling techniques

Activity 1.1
identifying channels

National Curriculum references

8b select and record observations and ideas, and research and organise a range of visual evidence and information, using a sketchbook
9a recognise the diverse methods and approaches used by artists, craftspeople and designers

Resources provided
Image Bank 1.1 (on a separate card):
Stills from BBC2 Idents
Image Bank 1.2:
Stills from MTV Idents
Information Sheet 1.1:
Idents
Video Clip 11:
BBC2 Idents

Resources required
Video player and monitor

You may wish to add to the resources provided by videotaping a selection of current idents (particularly seasonal idents, such as those promoting Christmas or Summer Season programming), or by collecting channel logos from television schedules in magazines.

Method
Invite the whole group to study Image Banks 1.1 and 1.2, Video Clip 11 and the resources you have gathered yourself. (Explain that the photographs on the Image Banks are stills taken from the television.)

Then begin the discussion on idents.

What are they? Where and when are they usually seen? What is their purpose? Which idents featured in the resource material have pupils seen before? Which ones do they prefer? How does the 'story' in each one work? What do they suggest (atmosphere/feelings)?

Then, working in pairs, and using sketchbooks for rough responses, pupils should focus on the meaning of about three individual images. Use the following questions to guide pupils' thoughts:

Lighting
▶ How is it used?
▶ How does it affect the meaning of the image?

Colour, texture and composition
▶ What colours are used in these images?
▶ What effect do these colours create?
▶ How are textures used to create an effect?
▶ How is the figure '2' in the BBC2 idents presented and positioned in relation to the other elements in the images? (Consider the MTV letters in the same way.)

Ask the whole group to read Information Sheet 1.1: Idents. Make sure pupils understand the function of idents, and the difference between specific and generic idents. Which of the examples on the Image Banks is a pure channel ident, and which offers the viewer something more, for example information about the drama being shown next?

End the activity by watching Video Clip 11 and reviewing the questions on lighting, colour, etc. Discuss the types and categories of channels. What type of channel is BBC2 (terrestrial, satellite or cable)? What type of programmes does it show, and what type of people watch it? Discuss the meaning of two or three BBC2 idents with the group. Discuss both the images and the soundtrack. Individual pupils might volunteer to explain their interpretations. Ask members of the group to describe, categorise and interpret other television idents that they have seen on satellite, cable or terrestrial channels.

Activity 1.2
into the schedule

National Curriculum references
9a recognise the diverse methods and approaches used by artists, craftspeople and designers
9b identify how visual elements are used to convey ideas, feelings and meanings in images and artefacts

Resources provided
Information Sheet 1.2:
Television Schedules
Image Bank 1.1 (on a separate card):
Stills from BBC2 Idents
Video Clip 12:
MTV Idents

Resources required
Video player and monitor; sketchbooks; drawing materials

Method
With the group, study Information Sheet 1.2, watch Video Clip 12 and discuss the following questions:

▶ Which of the idents in Video Clip 12 would fit into the MTV programme schedule provided? Where would they fit best?
▶ Which ones would you repeat often? (Why would you want to repeat them?)
▶ Which ones would you use sparingly?

Pupils should now look at the idents featured on Image Bank 1.1 (this is a separate card). Where would they best fit into the BBC2 Wednesday night schedule provided?

From the information given on Information Sheet 1.2, what would pupils say are the main differences between the two channels?

For a brief follow-up exercise or for homework, pupils could draw up one day's schedule for a channel they watch regularly. They should include one 'break' in the schedule where there are likely to be idents and trailers about the channel, and then go on to make rough drawings and notes about the sort of promotional information they think might be provided at that point. What do the presenters/announcers say, what do they look like and in what kind of setting are they presented? Which forthcoming programmes do they promote and how are these titles presented? Which images appear on the screen?

creating a channel
identity

Objectives *In Part 2, pupils will*

▶ learn more about the process of identifying and targeting an audience
▶ make preliminary plans/drawings for a new logo and ident for a fictional or existing television channel

▶ explore and experiment with design ideas and materials, examining in particular how the makers of idents have borrowed ideas from fine art

---

Activity 2.1

logos: size, shape and style

National Curriculum references

8c experiment with and select from visual and other source material to stimulate and develop ideas for independent work

8d select from and experiment with materials, images and ideas, and extend their experience of a range of materials, tools and techniques

Resources provided

Video Clip 11:
BBC2 Idents
Video Clip 12:
MTV Idents

Resources required

Video player and monitor

Ask pupils to collect examples of television channel logos from listings magazines, and to find product logos/symbols on packaging and in advertisements.

Method

Draw the logos/symbols used by the four main terrestrial channels and MTV on the board for all to see. Ask pupils to think about the shape and the style of the letters/numbers used. These questions will help to guide the discussion:

▶ How is each logo designed in terms of size, shape and style?
▶ What do these logos suggest about the character and style of each channel?
▶ Would a different typeface/size alter the way in which viewers think about a channel?

Watch Video Clips 11 and 12 and discuss how the logo is used in each ident:
▶ What does the BBC2 ident showing the '2' falling into the dust convey?
▶ How does sound enhance the movement of the logo in each film?

Activity 2.2

recycling art images

National Curriculum reference

9c relate art, craft and design to its social, historical and cultural context, e.g. identify codes and conventions used in different times and cultures

Resources provided

Video Clip 12:
MTV Idents
Image Bank 1.2:
MTV Ident – Art of All Ages

Resources required

Video player and monitor

Art books, posters or postcards featuring the work of a range of surrealist and avant-garde artists, for example Magritte, Duchamp and Dali. It would be helpful to have available colour reproductions of the paintings mentioned below under 'Method'.

Method

With the group, watch Video Clip 12 and study the idents which feature Magritte's *This is Not a Pipe*, Botticelli's *Spring* and Van Gogh's *Starry Night*. (See also the animated reference in the MTV ident to the film *Frankenstein*.)

Invite pupils to compare these filmed versions with the original images. They should consider how the film makers have borrowed from the work of famous painters who, at the time they were working, were considered innovative and unusual, perhaps even shocking.

Use the following questions to guide the ensuing discussion:
► In each case, what was the intention of the original artist?
► Within which style or tradition were these artists working?
► How do they convey meaning through symbols? What do their pictures mean?
► How have these abstract images been technically manipulated for use on television?
► What new meanings do they now possess?

Activity 2.3

inventing a new logo and ident

National Curriculum references

8c experiment with and select from visual and other source material to stimulate and develop ideas for independent work
9d identify how and why styles and traditions change over time and from place to place, recognising the contribution of artists, craftspeople and designers

Resources provided

Activity Sheet 2.1:
Inventing a New Logo and Ident

Resources required

Drawing materials; sketchbooks

Method

Work individually or in pairs. Using Activity Sheet 2.1, discuss the type of channel for which pupils would like to design a new logo and ident. (They can use the examples given or invent their own.)

They may want to choose a channel wholly devoted to films, for example.

Or they may prefer a channel which features mixed programming for a wider audience.

Once they have decided on the channel, its style and its likely audience, pupils should begin to think about the channel's logo. Does it feature words, letters or numbers? Is it a purely abstract design? Will viewers know what it means? Will it be instantly recognisable?

Pupils should now begin to discuss and draw rough ideas in their sketchbooks for their television ident film (to last between 10 and 20 seconds). They can design a specific or a generic ident; some may prefer to design a film that makes no reference to the channel's name, but they must convey/ represent the spirit of the channel as they see it. They have to bear in mind that the ident will be viewed frequently and it has to be distinctive.

Activity 2.4
2-D to 3-D

National Curriculum references

8e select from and interpret visual elements and realise their intentions in a range of media

8f modify and refine their work, and plan and make further developments in the light of their own and others' evaluations

Resources provided

Video Clip 10:
The City
Video Clip 12:
MTV Idents
Video Clip 13:
Gargantuan
Video Clip 14:
Sundial
Video Clip 15:
Eerie
Video Gallery (Module C) Part 2, Activity 2.4
Examples from pupils' work

Resources required

Computer equipment and software (see Technical Guide on p.70); video player and monitor; projection equipment; sketchbooks; drawing materials; work from Activity 2.3

Secondary sources such as books, magazines, photographs, films and posters which reflect different kinds of art.

Method

Pupils now consider how they will transform the rough sketches and notes they made in Activity 2.3 into a television ident. Discuss what technical and planning processes they will have to go through, and what resources and equipment they have available or will need in order to make their idents. At this stage, pupils experiment and prepare their ideas for final production. You may wish to show pupils the Video Gallery to give them some ideas.

Planning

Are pupils happy with the logos they have produced? They may like to investigate different ways of positioning and colouring the letters and figures in their logo, selecting a typeface that best conveys the image of the channel.

Storyboarding techniques can be used to help pupils plan their ident frame by frame. Pupils should select appropriate short musical excerpts and sound effects that can be faded up and down to accompany the sequence of images. Is there to be a voice-over? Will the announcer be male or female? What tone of voice will he or she use?

Into three dimensions

Familiarise pupils with the different media and materials they can use to bring their images to life:

▶ model sets, figures and puppets made, for example, from paper, card, wood, metal, clay, Plasticine, ceramics
▶ two- and three-dimensional collages using the materials already produced in Activity 2.3

▶ two-dimensional models and text scanned into a computer (Adobe Photoshop or Macromind Director software are useful here) and then animated
▶ three-dimensional models filmed (videoed) and processed into the computer; text and graphics added
▶ images produced and manipulated directly on the computer

It is worth giving pupils the chance to experiment with graphics and animation software and computer equipment before they commit their images to film.

Once the model sets or collages have been completed, pupils can take Polaroid photographs to record and evaluate the composition. What lighting techniques will they need to use? Do they want to create an impression of depth or of flatness? They can also incorporate the channel logo by projecting a slide of the symbol on to the background set, or material. Textures for a background can also be projected.

The Video Gallery shows examples of pupils' mixed media work influenced by other artists.

Abstract films

Some pupils may have elected to create an abstract ident that does not feature the channel name or logo, but which develops a theme or spirit for the channel in question. Video Clips 10 and 13–15 (all one-minute films) demonstrate how atmosphere and moods can be created.

producing a television
ident

Objectives *In Part 3, pupils will*

▶ produce their own television channel ident

▶ evaluate and modify the design in the light of audience responses

Activity 3.1:
producing the ident

National Curriculum reference
8e select from and interpret visual elements and realise their intentions in a range of media

Resources provided
Video Gallery (Module C) 3.1:
Video and stills from pupils' work
Video Gallery (Module C) 3.2:
Video and stills from pupils' work
Video Gallery (Module C) 3.3:
Video and stills from pupils' work
Video Gallery (Module C) 3.4:
Video and stills from pupils' work

Resources required
All material produced so far in Parts 1 and 2

Video camera; 16 mm film camera; video recorder; computer equipment and software, for example Adobe Photoshop or Macromind Director (see Technical Guide, p.70).

See also *Hands On, A Teacher's Guide to Media Technology* by Roy Stafford (BFI, 1993) for further information about animation and computer equipment. This accessible book provides a useful guide to classroom applications.

Method
Using the work they have produced so far in this module, pupils can now proceed to make their short films.

The group may like to look at the Video Gallery again to study the approach taken by other pupils. Video Gallery 3.1 shows video and stills of pupils working on BBC1, BBC2 and MTV logos. Video Gallery 3.2 shows stills of pupils involved in computer animation work. Video Gallery 3.3 shows stills of work in ceramics. Video Gallery 3.4 shows stills of sets and props which are ready to be animated on computer or 16 mm film.

Where appropriate, help pupils to use computer software to scan in two-dimensional work and to input video clips, if you have access to the necessary equipment. From that point, pupils can add text and sound to produce a good quality product.

If pupils are using 16 mm film to animate their models, puppets or paper figures, then they can also transfer their sequences to video for further treatment via computer animation, and textual and graphics overlay.

Once the sequences have been filmed, pupils can place their idents between real programmes on a pre-recorded videotape to see how they would work in a broadcasting context. Or they can simply play them back to an audience, presenting the films as demo tapes of their new television idents (as a design consultant or an advertising agency might).

Activity 3.2

presentation, review and modification

National Curriculum references

8f modify and refine their work and plan and make further developments in the light of their own and others' evaluations

9e express ideas and opinions and justify preferences using knowledge and an art, craft and design vocabulary

Resources required

Pupils' own work – all sketchbook material, preparatory drawings and notes, finished models/artwork, finished idents

Method

First, the group should play back/ present their finished idents to an audience and explain the intended purpose behind each film.

(The idents can be inserted between real programmes on a pre-recorded videotape to see how they would work in a broadcasting context. Alternatively, they can be presented alone, maybe as the 'demo tapes' produced by the channel's 'Art Department'.)

From the moment they began to design their idents, pupils should have had a certain type of viewer in mind (for example, retired couples or children under five). Refer pupils back to Activity Sheet 2.1: Inventing a New Logo and Ident. It would be helpful if the group could now arrange to show their films to individuals from the relevant 'targeted' audience (maybe members of a University of the Third Age group, or infants from the local nursery school). If this is not possible, pupils can present their idents to their peers.

In either case, the audience should be encouraged to give comments. Does each ident fulfil its purpose? Is its meaning clear? Is it appropriate to the chosen season/time of day/audience?

Pupils may like to formalise the evaluation stage by preparing oral presentations or written reports on the work involved in producing their idents. They may even wish to video or tape interviews with each other about the design process.

Once all the feedback has been received, pupils can assess their work and maybe modify their idents, either by refilming certain sections or, alternatively, by reflecting the changes in a written or spoken evaluation.

Teachers should base their evaluation of pupils' work on the criteria provided in the Assessment Table on the following page. The Learning Outcomes specified in the table can be related to National Curriculum criteria for Investigation and Making, and Knowledge and Understanding.

assessment
table

Learning outcomes	Activities	Evidence	Assessment methods
Categorise, analyse and produce imitations, or original TV idents or short films, for a specific audience	Part 1: Activity 1.1 Part 2: Activity 2.1; 2.2 Part 3: Activity 3.1	Range of visual research and written notes in the sketchbook, from different sources	Evaluation of product(s)
Assess the way TV idents borrow from other art/media forms	Part 2: Activity 2.2	Oral discussion; written notes	Question and discussion
Apply video, film and animation techniques; combine with traditional art media forms and techniques, such as drawing, painting, typography, ceramics and puppetry	Part 2: Activity 2.4 Part 3: Activity 3.1	Practical experiments/proposals	Evaluation of product(s)
Demonstrate knowledge of composition: *mise-en-scène*, perspective, lighting, colour, camera movement, framing and angle	Part 2: Activity 2.2; 2.4 Part 3: Activity 3.1	Sketchbook; loose design sheets, showing development of ideas	Evaluation of product(s)
Reflect and modify media products in the light of responses from real audiences	Part 3: Activity 3.1; 3.2	Visual and written notes in the sketchbook; final product(s)	Evaluation of sketchbook
Evaluate the different roles in the television production process	Parts 1, 2 and 3	Pupil self-assessment	Question and discussion

idents

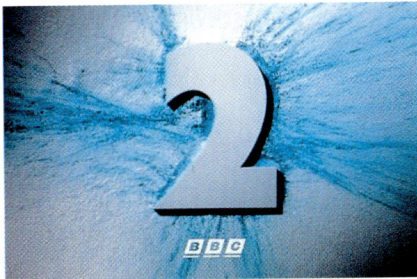

Idents

Idents are the short 'films' or animations that link television programmes. They provide between-programme continuity.

Logo

Idents tell the viewers which channel they are watching (often by showing the channel's *logo*, such as the blue '2' for BBC2) and they also help to announce the programme coming next. Such information may be conveyed in an indirect fashion, through visual clues. For example, the Channel 4 logo is sometimes combined with the image of an American baseball helmet to show viewers that they can expect a sports programme to follow.

Idents have to be short (so as not to use up too much precious broadcasting time), to the point and easily understood. The makers of these films have to create a strong image or brand for their channel that will be memorable and they often borrow ideas from other sources, for example well-known paintings.

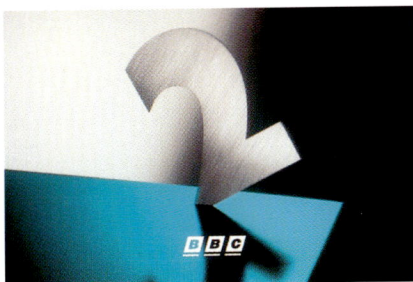

Generic idents

There are various types of ident. Generic idents usually feature the channel's logo and can be inserted between any two programmes at any time. Their job is to brand and identify the channel.

Animations also provide between-programme linking, or continuity (for example, the gun, the carrot). They make use of the digit '2', but they do not lead into the programme: they come at the start of trailers or at the end, or both! In animations, the '2' is smaller and is frequently played around with – the viridian blue is never used.

Specific idents

Specific idents, however, are used to remind viewers that they are watching a special season or evening of programming. It might be a 'Love Night' for Valentine's Day (film featuring a heart), or a '*Film Noir* Season' (ident showing shadows, venetian blinds, a book of pulp fiction stories). In specific idents, the channel's usual logo and music may not be used.

Many idents are quite abstract and contain no trace of the channel's name or number. These films are designed to give a particular feel or look to the channel.

Trailers

Idents should not be confused with *trailers*. Trailers are longer promotional films that advertise specific programmes that are to be screened later, maybe several days or weeks ahead. Idents are more immediate. They relate to the channel you are watching *now*.

television schedules

WEDNESDAY

MTV	
6.30	The Grind (*Weekly show featuring nightclub music and celebrity guests*)
7.00	3 from 1 (*Three videos by the same artist or on the same theme*)
7.15	Awake on the Wildside (*Breakfast music magazine programme*)
8.00	VJ Maria (*Video jockey – broad range of music*)
11.00	The Soul of MTV (*Soul, reggae and funk music programme with Radio 1 DJ Lisa I'Anson*)
12.00	Greatest Hits (*Show featuring music videos by innovative artists. Commentary by VJ*)
1.00	Music Non-Stop (*Featuring latest music hits*)
2.00	3 from 1

BBC2	
6.20	Open University – Social Cognition (*Adult Education*)
6.45	Open University – Arts. Fontainebleau (*Adult Education*)
7.35	Poetry and Landscape in the 18th Century (*Adult Education*)
8.00	Breakfast News
8.15	Patrik Postcard (*cartoon*)
8.40	Conan the Adventurer (*cartoon*)
9.05	Cousteau's Amazon (*Nature programme with Jacques Cousteau*)
9.50	Holiday Outings (*Travel-based programme*)
10.00	Making Tracks (*Documentary series about railways around the world*)
10.30	Camp Wilder (*US comedy series about a house full of teenagers*)
10.55	Film: You'll Find Out (D Butler, 1940, US)
12.30	Working Lunch (*Business news*)
1.00	Forget-Me-Not Farm (*Live action and animated children's programme*)
2.10	Songs of Praise (*Hymns and prayers from a parish church*)

3.00	Cinematic	3.00	News, Local News, Weather, followed by
	(*Daily 15 minute slot – information on*		Man on the Rim (*Documentary looking at the*
	current film and home video releases)		*Pacific's first migrants*)
3.15	Hanging out with Enrico (*Daily programme*		
	which answers viewers' enquiries and gives a		
	brief overview of MTV programmes)	3.55	News, Local News, Weather
4.00	News at Night (*News*)	4.00	Film: The Dark at the Top of the Stairs
4.30	Dial MTV		(D Mann, 1960, US)
5.00	The Zig and Zag Show		
5.30	Hanging out with Enrico		
		6.00	Star Trek: The New Generation (*Cult sci-fi*
			drama series)
		6.45	Natural Born Footballers (*Short series on*
			famous footballers)
7.00	Greatest Hits	7.00	The Bomb: Hiroshima
			(*VJ Day commemorative series*)
8.00	Most Wanted (*Live programme featuring guest*	8.00	The Day That Changed My Life
	performers and a studio audience)		(*Documentary series looking at the day that*
			changed a person's life)
		8.30	Delia Smith's Summer Collection
			(*Cookery series*)
		9.00	The Travel Show
9.30	Beavis and Butthead (*US cartoon*)	9.30	Africa's Big Game (*Nature programme*)
10.00	News at Night		
10.15	Cinematic		
		10.20	Watch Out (*Nature programme looking at*
			British wildlife)
10.30	The State (*Weekly comedy sketch show*	10.30	Newsnight (*News/discussion*)
	presented by 11-man New York troupe)		
11.00	The End? (*Magazine featuring cartoons,*		
	pop videos and chat)	11.15	Over the Edge
			(*Magazine series for disabled people*)
		11.45	Animation Now (*Animation series*)
		11.55	Weatherview
		12.00	Modelling in the Long Term (*Educational*
			programme – part of The Learning Zone)
12.30	Night Videos	12.25	Making Medical Decisions (*Educational*
			programme – part of The Learning Zone)
5.00–6.30	Awake on the Wildside		

inventing a new
logo and ident

You have been asked to invent a new logo design for a television channel (real or imaginary) and then to make a short ident film (between 10 and 20 seconds long) for that channel.

Channel

First choose your channel. You can use any of the ones you may watch already (maybe BBC1, BBC2, ITV, Channel 4, S4C, UTV, Scottish TV, MTV), you can invent your own, or you can choose from one of the following suggestions:

▶ A Nature channel (showing wildlife and natural history programmes)
▶ An Astronomy channel
▶ A Shopping channel
▶ A Sports channel
▶ A Movie channel

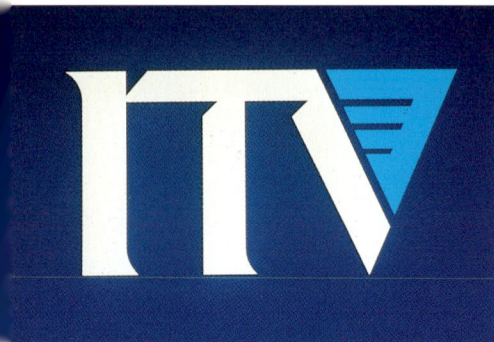

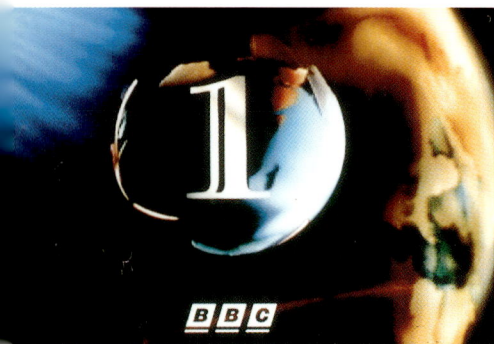

Logo

Now you can start thinking about the logo or symbol that will identify that channel. Think about the name you will give your channel if it doesn't have one already. Most existing channel use letters and/or numbers to form their logos.

There are other points to consider when devising your logo and ident:

▶ What sort of programmes will your channel show?
▶ Who will be watching it:
   children (0–5)?
   teenagers (12–16)?
   families with children (5–10)?
   youth (16–24)?
   older adults (40–55)?
▶ Will it be a regional or a national channel?
▶ Will the logo be on screen all the time? If so, it shouldn't be too intrusive or take up too much space.
▶ How adaptable or flexible will your logo have to be? For example, if you are designing a logo for a sports channel, will it have to incorporate visual clues about a variety of sports programmes?
▶ Will there be logos from commercial sponsors to include, e.g. Nike, Sprite, etc.?

Try to ensure that your logo and ident convey the right image for your channel and that they are appropriate for the audience you want to attract.

Ident

Now start to draft out some ideas for your ident film, bearing in mind that it should, if possible, feature the channel's logo.

Think about when the ident is to be shown. Which of the following will you choose?

▶ Breakfast (0700–0900)
▶ Midday (1200–1400)
▶ Afternoon (1400–1600)
▶ Children's TV (1600–1800)
▶ Adult TV (2030 onwards)
▶ Spring, Summer, Autumn or Winter

Does your ident accompany a trailer? Is it a specific or a generic ident?

Which kind of programme does it appear before/after? Choose from this list:

▶ Sports
▶ Sitcom
▶ Consumer
▶ Soap
▶ Documentary
▶ Magazine programme on daytime TV
▶ Breakfast

Or maybe you can think of some other kinds of programme that are more appropriate to your particular channel?

Finally, think about the music soundtrack. What mood or tune suits your ident? Experiment with different ideas, matching the length of the piece of music to the image sequence.

mtv ident –
art
of all ages

Channels like MTV aim to please a music loving or culture hungry audience by using witty and sophisticated idents.

Top left:
Egyptian 3D
Top right:
Starry Night –
Van Gogh
Bottom left:
Sistine Chapel ceiling
– Michelangelo
Bottom right:
Classical 3D

technical
guide

Computers

Many schools use Acorn A300 series computers with Genesis software. This enables pupils to combine photographic and drawn images with text, sound and graphics to produce multimedia presentations.

Other systems and packages are available. Adobe Photoshop software (used with Apple Mac computers) is simple to operate and provides possibilities for image manipulation, from simple cut and paste commands to the rendering of lighting effects on an image. Macromind Director authoring software is also very effective.

Digitiser

By linking a digitiser to a computer, still images can be downloaded or grabbed directly from a camera, video or SVC (still video camera) and converted into image files. The equipment is relatively cheap and allows pupils to transfer images directly from video on to the computer and then to print them out on ordinary paper. Similarly, a scanner will 'process' a photograph or other printed image and convert that into computer data.

Graphics

It is necessary to have a colour monitor in order to benefit fully from a graphics package, and a PC will need to be fitted with a graphics card. It should also be noted that graphics are not available on all Apple Mac machines. The Amiga and the Atari are configured for graphics and are the easiest machines to set up.

Graphics require a great deal of memory, especially if you wish to animate objects. The more complicated the image (for example, in terms of the number of different colours used), the more information the computer needs to process.

Animation

Unfortunately, most camcorders and VCRs have one major drawback when compared to cine-cameras or computers – they cannot be used for single-frame shooting. With a standard camcorder, it is virtually impossible to emulate 'cel technique' (i.e. the recording of single frames to make up an animated sequence) unless your pupils have the necessary dexterity and infinite patience to start and stop the pause control with great accuracy. The results can be very jerky. Some domestic camcorders are said to possess ainmation features, but these have not been used very widely so far. However, basic animation techniques are possible with most machines. Computer animation is more precise and easier to sequence.

Alternatively, a semi-professional video animation suite is available. This is used by several animation artists and could be bought by schools for around £1000.

Probably the most satisfactory and instructive method is to use a 16 mm cine-camera together with a tripod and floodlights.

Desk top video (DTV)

This is another video production technique which does not involve the camera or VCR at the creative stage. A small group of two or three pupils could work on titles or graphics while others are recording material, logging, storyboarding, etc. You will need a computer, a genlock, a monitor (which needs a video input), a VCR and tape, titling software such as TVText and a formatted disk to save the results. A simple television ident can easily be created using this equipment. If you have a paint program, for example DPaint, pupils may be able to add extra features (blood dripping from the horror title!) or to design their own font.